The Englishwoman's House

The Duchess of Devonshire's bedroom at Chatsworth House.

The Englishwoman's House

Edited by Alvilde Lees-Milne
Photographed by Derry Moore

Fontana/Collins
Grafton Street, London, W1
1985

Designed and produced by Breslich & Foss
Middlesex House
34–42 Cleveland Street
London WIP 5FB
Designer: Tony Garrett

First published by William Collins Sons and Co. Ltd 1984
First issued by Fontana Paperbacks 1985
Text and Design © Breslich & Foss
Photographs © Derry Moore

Set by Fakenham Photosetting Ltd, Fakenham, Norfolk
Originated by Dot Gradations Ltd, Essex
and printed by Grijelmo, Spain

Endpapers: *Fabric 'Khayyham' reproduced by courtesy of
Arthur Sanderson and Sons Ltd, Berners Street, London.*

Contents

Foreword by HRH
Princess Michael of Kent

As a very un-Englishwoman I feel privileged to have been asked to write a foreword to this book.

I am, however, lucky enough to live in two quintessential English houses, Nether Lypiatt Manor in Gloucestershire and a part of Kensington Palace on four floors. Both are full of English furniture, legacies of my husband's grandmother, Queen Mary, an adoptive Englishwoman with legendary taste and knowledge of the decorative arts; and my late father-in-law, Prince George, Duke of Kent, who shared his mother's passion for collecting.

I have always disliked the term 'decoration' and have carefully contrived to have any house I have lived in not looking 'decorated'. The English houses, many of them included in this book, that I most admire have successfully avoided the stamp of a particular designer and instead reflect their owners' taste, fantasy, whims and way of life.

Nearly twenty years ago I came to England to study, in particular, the eighteenth century English house, and so I hope I have restored both our houses in a style to which they were once accustomed. If only this book had been written sooner many of the mysteries of the English house would have been unfolded to me much earlier.

Marie Christine

A mirror in Barbara Cartland's house reflecting and surrounded by many of the original paintings for covers of her novels.

Introduction

Today one has to be cautious in discriminating between the sexes. Men and women are supposed to share the same sensitivities and sensibilities. Nevertheless, when it comes to a house, women do as a rule show a livelier interest than men in making it attractive. They also have a more positive approach in its arrangement.

So-called women of taste in the 1920s and 1930s were rather frightened of colour. They were inclined to favour pastel shades, beige and *eau de Nil*, which they considered safe and respectable backgrounds. Today all this has changed. As in cooking, stronger flavours prevail.

The purpose of this book is to demonstrate how twenty-eight women have coped with the different problems of creating homes for themselves and their families, while revealing their candid likes and dislikes in decoration.

The decision whom to invite to contribute to the book has not been an easy one. I have tried to collect different types of houses, large and small, in town and country. Each owner has written about her favourite rooms and objects with genuine affection. Indeed, enthusiasm seems to be the keynote of every chapter.

The contributors take us on a personally conducted tour, sometimes only to one room, sometimes to several. They regale us with personal anecdotes and explain the multifarious problems which beset them. Some of these are amusing. All of them are instructive and provide us with ingenious hints and practical advice how to set about creating our own homes when that critical moment of life comes, which it inevitably must, to all of us.

This is a book of constructive thought and original ideas. Some contributors have had to modernise large, stately homes untouched for years; others have reconstituted old rectories and cottages of various dates and styles. Others have tackled London flats, and one has even adapted an old dairy. They all have something different to tell us. Whether you admire their taste, or not, you cannot fail to be intrigued by the diversity of their ideas. The reader can really feel that he or she gets inside the houses, and furthermore to know the writers individually. Their personalities come through so forcibly.

I wish to thank Her Royal Highness Princess Michael of Kent, whose interest in interior decoration is well known, for writing the Foreword. I am also of course deeply grateful to all those whose splendid cooperation and patience have made this book what it is.

Thilde Lees-Milne

Soft aquamarine and apricot are used in the little Regency sitting-room, decorated as a print-room.

Laura Ashley

RHYDOLDOG HOUSE
Rhayador, Powys

R hydoldog means water running over stones. This could either be a reference to the two beautiful waterfalls which tumble for two hundred feet down the hill behind the house, or perhaps to some stepping stones across the streams which flow through the pastures below. One of the streams was diverted over two hundred years ago and the bed made into an impressive driveway lined with cedars in place of the old farm cart track which approached from behind the hill.

In fact the house, like most old buildings, has seen lots of changes, even in this case to the extent of moving the front entrance to face three different directions in three different centuries.

Rhydoldog was built in the seventeenth century as a group of stone farm buildings with a farmhouse comprising living-room, dairy and bedrooms above. The front door faced into the hill for shelter and also for the convenience of running across the yard to the extensive farm buildings. Early in the eighteenth century the story goes that a group of smugglers from Kent, fleeing the Customs men, came with their families to hide in the Welsh hills. One of them bought Rhydoldog farm

The drawing-room is mainly crimson; the original grey marble fire-place and mirrored overmantel have been put back.

and turned the little house back to front to give a Georgian façade with the additions of dining-room, sitting-room, an elegant staircase, some more bedrooms and a good wine cellar. Most importantly, the front door now faced the view down the Wye valley, and with the new carriage-way made from diverting the river bed one could sweep in style right up to the new front terrace.

Then at the end of the nineteenth century another great change took place when the house was turned around once again to face north east by putting a new Gothic porch at the side, a new entrance hall with stained glass doors, encaustic patterned tiles, a gun-room, flower-room, library and brand-new large drawing-room. Upstairs, there were now dressing-rooms and eleven bed-rooms plus a large schoolroom.

When our family took over the house in 1971 it was in a very good state of repair and we were fortunate in that the same local building firm had looked after it as long as anyone could remember, so that they knew exactly where all the various pipes and electrical fittings, boilers, etc., were. We just had to get down to the redecoration of all the rooms.

My own attitude towards decorating an old house is to find out all one can about the history of the house and even, if possible, the original colours used. I have no prejudices about colour but prefer to stand in a room and feel what it is asking for, especially insofar as its original build-ing date is concerned. This house, however, was a complete mix of old Welsh farmhouse, Georgian, and finally and probably dominantly, Victorian Gothic. The only answer was to decorate each room exactly to its own period, and this we did.

The first hallway is Victorian and is wall-papered with an Owen Jones print coloured in browns and greys to match the old tiles and blend-ing with the lines of old books on the shelves and on into the library, which is in plums and bur-gundy on cream with curtains in a paisley stripe and a faded rose carpet. The heart of the house, with its elegant early eighteenth century staircase and polished oak floor, is wallpapered in a Regency stripe in soft aquamarine and apricot; these colours follow through into the little Regency sitting-room, which is decorated as a very fashionable looking print-room. The wallpaper here is a moiré print which gives the effect of fabric on the wall and the striped curtains have a zigzag

A pretty bedroom looks over the Wye Valley.

pelmet taken from one of the rooms at the Brigh-ton Pavilion. Through the green baize door into the back hallway, which has not very much light, there is white linoleum and a pale grey and white wallpaper to give maximum light effect. The large old kitchen itself has terracotta/cream 'Shepherd's Purse' wallpaper and curtains which look very nice with the scrubbed tables and tiled floor and cook-ing range. The dairy and laundry follow through mainly in creams with touches of terracotta.

The dining-room started its life as a Georgian room with a fire-place of the period flanked with arched open shelves for china displays. Then at the turn of the century an Edwardian bay was added with large glass doors to the terrace. We decided to decorate it in Edwardian style with a wonderful old wallpaper print of the period in deep browns with matching curtains. Very dark you might say, yet in candlelight with a brightly burning fire it is stunning and in summer it looks cool and makes a frame for the wonderful view.

However, it was the drawing-room which gave the greatest challenge. It was not as if the house as it stood was an architectural masterpiece (people have actually burst out laughing at the sight of it), and so it was very straightforward to obtain planning permission for what I had in mind—to take out the ugly drawing-room win-dows and build a conservatory right along the terrace. It seemed strange in fact that the house hadn't got a conservatory already and now that it

Stepping down from the drawing-room into the conservatory.

has everyone imagines it has always been there, it looks so right. So I used our local builders, gave them my plans, which were a composite of all the Gothic style conservatories I had ever seen, and we tiled the floor, made doors for each end with low handles which were a copy of our front door handle and shaped the roof and windows to suit. We discovered a company who were reproducing iron seats to an old pattern and after that it was no problem to add a riot of ferns, lilies, palms and aspidistras as well as a statue and other pieces of sculpture. The upholstery, cushions, tiles, etc., are in an Owen Jones print in a fresh green and white. This conservatory was one of the most satisfying things I have ever done and was especially poignant for me because I knew I was going to have to leave the house very soon afterwards.

But we mustn't forget the drawing-room,

Another part of the drawing-room with Gothic bookcase.

The Gothic style conservatory looks as if it had always been part of the house.

which now looked totally a part of the conservatory since one stepped straight down from it. Naturally it had to be decorated in Gothic style and seemed to want to be crimson (although I still long to do a room in Gothic blue and gold). A friend of mine possessed a very ancient rug which both of us loved but was really in tatters. So we persuaded a carpet company to reproduce the same design and its border in a smart Brussels weave, keeping the original colouring of shades of crimson on a sand background. This looked magnificent when laid in our drawing-room. We had at the same time put back the original heavy grey marble fire-place and mirrored overmantel and removed from the room every stick of furniture, which consisted of the usual eclectic mix of comfortable sofas and family paraphernalia (because you have to be singleminded when decorating and I do know about sulking husbands and children, etc.). A huge Gothic side table was the first find and it cost so little money that the family groans became even louder. Then a splendid bookcase was installed plus extraordinary chairs that most people wouldn't want, some antlers for the wall, various feathers and shells under glass domes, more sculptured heads of poets and politicians, and the room looked magnificent. I forgot to mention that the wallpaper is printed in the same colourings as the carpet and was from an old design found at Harewood House in Yorkshire; the motif for the curtains came from the footboard of an old bed and the design for the pelmets was copied from an old upholsterer's book. I am particularly fond of these old tradesmen's books and the very elaborate, quite theatrical interior designs they portray—and why not live with swags and tassels? Anyway, the drawing-room now looks distinctly like the interior of a hunting lodge in a Walter Scott novel.

For seven years I lived between this Welsh house and a family house in London and I left Rhydoldog for ever on an early April day when the wild daffodils were smothering the banks of the old water garden and thousands more nodded to me all the way down the lovely driveway to say farewell.

I now live in Brussels and in France in quite a different way, but that is another story altogether.

Laura Ashley

Gothic side table in the drawing-room. ☞

Ana Ines Astor

A Cottage
Wiltshire

A few years ago, I needed to find a house in the country large enough to have children and grandchildren to stay, easy to look after, in nice country and in pleasant surroundings.

Having looked at endless unsuitable places and been 'gazumped' whenever there was anything vaguely adaptable, I was about to give up when I happened to look at some old copies of *Country Life*. There, staring out at me, was the cottage I needed. It looked charming, unspoilt, with all the necessary requirements, and the price was extremely attractive. But the fact that it had

remained unsold for many weeks made me uneasy. There must be some terrible drawback. I found out that the problem was a right of way, which led from one end of the village to the other, allowing people and riders to go by at all times. But this 'drawback' has been a pleasure for me—I enjoy people walking by and riders returning from the local hunt, but *they* must be plagued by my unending swearing, in every language I know, as I struggle in my garden. At one time the right of way became one of the most popular dog lavatories within two miles. It has now been gravelled, and

The Garden Room.

this seems to be the answer.

The cottage is thatched, with very thick walls and low ceilings, and is about three hundred years old. There were some additional buildings at the back which I have since joined to the centre building. It had originally been a pub, overlooking the village green. One of the downstairs bedrooms had a bread oven, a large beam going across the ceiling with three very strong hooks, and, when the workmen started putting the heating in, they found a well at the far corner of the room, by the window. It had to be filled in, but I did regret it the summer of that terrible drought.

The house had a happy feeling about it and you could sense that the previous owners had loved it and been content there; and there were no inglenook fire-places.

A tiresome friend, now a firm acquaintance, remarked that it was rather 'twee'. 'What a joy', said I, 'then I can fill the garden with gnomes and put "private eye" faces on them.' Undeterred by gloomy friends, I settled down to organise it. Taste is not only personal but relative. As a rule, houses have characters of their own which dictate how they would like you to live in them—that is unless they are irretrievably uncooperative.

It took a long time, sitting in every room at different angles and in different lights, plans in hand, studying all features and adapting them to taste and needs. Still sensitive to the 'twee' remark, contemplating what small proportions I had to work with, I decided then and there to turn it into a sort of nursery cottage. Not being British by origin, I could not aspire to the perfection of a Mrs. Tiggywinkle ambience so decided to try for the third bear style. A rather feminine third bear.

There were lots of alterations to be done, outside and inside. One of them was integrating an upstairs bathroom which I took off the end of a very long bedroom. As the ceiling below seemed tired and sagging, I was advised by the local builder to put in a plastic bath-tub to alleviate the burden. With a plastic bath-tub you tend to lose the heat of the water; and if you have a large guest you inevitably hear, as the walls are thin upstairs, a funny noise of body rubbing against wet plastic, sounding a bit like a seal.

I have never used an interior decorator. I came to this country during the war when there were none to be had, so followed my own taste, making endless mistakes as I went. In my time, I have tortured many builders. I always believe in using local professionals and started with the most expensive, as there was a lot of rewiring to be done and heating to be installed. A few years later, when I joined the outbuildings to the main house, I thought I would be clever and do it on the cheap. Felled by the charm of a man whose magic words were of how everything was possible and could be done immediately, I gave in, only to find a few years later that I had to go back to the expensive one as the roof leaked and the windows and doors rotted.

The entrance hall had to be altered so that a large larder could be integrated into it, so I had to get the right proportions in order to house gum-boots, baskets and the general paraphernalia of winter outdoor wear. Being in a hurry to move in, I chose to whitewash all walls. I found, in a town nearby, very nice carpeting in an off-white,

A pen-and-ink drawing of the back of the cottage by Mrs. Astor.

smooth tweed easy to shampoo, and I used it for all the downstairs rooms.

The sitting-room faces south. Two large thick beams run all the length of the room, under the ceiling, from fire-place to the opposite wall; these beams were supported by an upright wooden post. As the ceiling sags, I was advised by the builders to add another supporting post in the middle of the room, about two feet from the other one. It was then difficult to know what to do with the awkward space between them, so I placed a small round table there and covered it with a patchwork cloth of different patterns of red, pink, greens, blues and pale blues on a white back-ground. On this table I placed a lamp which lights up the centre of the room. In between the win-dows, facing south, I put a desk, and on the oppo-site side a large and long settee to seat large-sized bears. The big stone fire-place had a Breughel look about it but the cold wind invariably howled down and it always smoked. I installed an old-fashioned iron wood-burner, called the 'Resolute'. It is effective, clean and warms a great deal of the house.

The curtains are hung by rings from plain dark wooden poles. I have used a very old-fashioned chintz, unobtainable now, of moss rose buds with green leaves on a white background speckled with light brown spots, and these are edged on the side facing the light in bright pink. The same chintz covers the large settee. By the fire-place under the window, there is a smaller settee covered in 'Amanda' Jonelle cotton, the overall colours of pale green and pink blending in with the rest of the room. I like mixing different prints in the same room, providing they have something in common, and have gone as far as covering an armchair with three different samples

The small window on the stairs is fitted with late Victorian stained glass.

The chairs and sofas in the sitting-room are covered in a mixture of gaily-coloured prints.

Mrs. Astor's bedroom.

The beamed sitting-room with south-facing windows.

I had bought to try out. It makes everything more varied and fun. All sofas and armchairs have needlework cushions with flower, butterfly or animal motifs, all colours and shapes blending into the room. By the fire-place there is a flowered bell-pull in needlework, and all side tables are white and low. Over the very large sofa there is a Venetian mirror, falling to pieces but still holding a lively reflection of the French door going into the garden. All paintings are done either by myself or members of my family. I do not have anything of value.

Sometimes in a room there is what I call the

Bermuda triangle, a fatal bit which will not come off, no matter how much you move the furniture around. There is one at the side of this room where I have two bookcases; in between the books I have photographs, bits of china and paintboxes. I am a clutterer by nature—much as I try to keep a room clear, within twenty-four hours it is full to the brim again.

A Venetian mirror hangs over the large sofa in the sitting-room.

By the fire-place on the left, there is a door which leads to a winding staircase. Halfway up there is a small window. My daughter gave me some stained glass from a church, late Victorian in alternating squares, some with primroses, others with cyclamen, with a deep red and green surround; it just fitted and looks very attractive.

The stairs are a bit narrow. They were painted black, and at night the light isn't too good. After a few falls it was obvious I had to sacrifice local norms for practicability, so I vandalised the stairs. I asked our local decorator to paint them

and the passage upstairs flamingo pink. It has created a great deal of comment, it gives the place some life, and I never fall now.

The bedrooms upstairs have very large beams going across and at an angle; they too were painted black. When I had the cracks in the walls done I painted all the beams white and it instantly made the rooms larger. I wallpapered walls and ceiling in a tiny, pale green flowered print on a white ground; you barely notice the print and it gives an overall colour without driving you mad. The paper came from Tesco's, and I have it in other bedrooms in different colours contrasting with the colours of the curtains. One particular bedroom has the curtains, dressing table, bed and buttoned Victorian armchair all covered in a Jonelle cotton named 'Loreta'; it is printed all over in different shades of reds and pinks relieved by a little pale green. The flowers have a distinct Eastern feeling. There is a square needlework rug with a deep pink background and a crown of white flowers in the middle with white initials inside it. All carpets upstairs are off-white. To give the bed some protection from the door I have hung from the ceiling, on a thick, round, brass rod, a curtain which runs round the foot of the bed. The chest-of-drawers is painted white and stencilled in a design of leaves in bright pink. I have used this design in different ways, alternating up and down, and it now looks very dressy, ready to go to a party. In this bedroom and in the passageway I have hung paintings by my grandchildren and children when they were young. I find them colourful, funny and artistic.

I don't think one's taste really changes; it expands as one acquires better ideas, through living. The cottage was decorated in two stages —when I first moved in and about six years later, when it needed repairs. By then my life was more relaxed and I had learnt many lessons.

We live in peace with each other—I love it. My cottage is my castle.

Chiquita Astor

Isabel Colegate

MIDFORD CASTLE
Bath, Avon

Our house is built in the shape of a clover-leaf, or trefoil. A magazine article in 1899 suggested that it was the ace of clubs, and that the original owner, Mr. Henry Disney Roebuck, had won a fortune on the turn of a card and commemorated it by having a house built for him in the shape of the winning card. It seems more likely that a fortunate inheritance from a rich uncle provided the wherewithal and that the design was taken from the *Builders Magazine* of 1774. In this John Carter, a Gothic enthusiast who had made various drawings of Horace Walpole's 'small cap-ricious house' at Strawberry Hill, published a plan for 'A Gothic Mansion to be Erected on an Eminence that Commands an Extensive Prospect'. The ground plan of Midford follows John Carter's, though the builder who carried out the design added a storey and enlarged the basement.

There are three rooms round a central diamond-shaped hall. The pattern is repeated on the two upper floors, with landings in place of the hall. The stairs go up one of the straight sides between the turrets in a kind of square spiral. It is a surprisingly practical and convenient design.

The castle from the north-east side.

The library showing the tall pointed windows.

Part of the hall.

Over the library fire-place the imaginary eighteenth-century landscape by Richard Bampfylde.

Less practical and convenient is the basement on which the whole thing is raised, and which extends in front of the house, underneath the strip of lawn and the balustrade, to emerge at ground level further down the hill. So determined was Mr. Disney Roebuck to build his house on just that slope of the steep hill that it had to be raised up on this strange platform, underneath which the servants, kitchens, horses and carriages were originally housed in what must have been, for the humans at least, some discomfort. Mr. Disney Roebuck secured his extensive prospect; the view over the Midford valley is essential to any idea of the house.

To one side of the house, and slightly lower, is a picturesque building put up about thirty years after the main house in order to accommodate the horses and carriages, and by that time the priest, in more comfort than the basement could afford. The Conolly family who bought the house in about 1810 were Roman Catholics, and at right angles to the stables they built a chapel whose tower remains although its walls have crumbled; the ruins have become incorporated in the garden. This building, like the view, is part of the effect of Midford. Like the house itself it is a curious mixture of fantasy and common sense.

None of the rooms in the house is large, although they are high. They all have pretty plasterwork on the ceilings and cornices. When we came to decorate the dining-room we thought of a

dusty yellow colour, but when we considered the ceiling and the cornice we felt we should never be able to decide how to do it and what to pick out in what colour, so we asked the decorator Peter Hood to help us. He dug back through the layers of paint and found the original colour. It was dusty yellow, a colour much used in eighteenth century Bath, he told us, because it was supposed to go well with Bath stone. He painted the ceiling in paler tones, picked out the cornice in terracotta and painted the woodwork flat white and grey. To make it perfect we still have to aspire to the red curtains he recommended for us.

I spend a good deal of my time in the library, where my desk is. The other room on the ground floor used to be the drawing-room. The kitchen is to the side of the house, a fairly discreet stone box which was built on in 1938, when the basement kitchen must have been finally pronounced too

A view of the nineteenth-century Chapel Tower through a quatrefoil of the castle.

inconvenient. The drawing-room is known to us as the orange room because when we first came we painted it that colour (there used to be a book of historic colours which you could get from Parsons Paints, and this as far as I remember was Majolica Yellow). In those days it was a children's room. The children are nearly all grown-up now but the room doesn't seem to have become any tidier; it is certainly nothing so decorous as a drawing-room.

From the tidiness point of view, the disadvantage of my having my desk in the library is outweighed by the fact that underneath the

The diamond-shaped hall looking through to the dining-room.

original glass-fronted bookcases on each side of the room are capacious recesses which look like drawers but are much deeper because of the thickness of the stone walls. Great heaps of papers of various kinds can be swept into these at a moment's notice; eventually, if left there long enough, they may be eaten by the mice. The bookcases presented us with what we thought was a problem. We wanted more book space but were nervous of diminishing or somehow throwing off balance the existing bookcases. Eventually we decided to put up the plainest possible shelves painted the same colour as the walls, and we had the ones between the windows made first. Even so, it was some time before we asked Alex Roberts to make the other two; as soon as they were up we wondered what we had been worrying about.

Alex Roberts is a furniture designer who lives and works in part of the stables here, and he has made several pieces of furniture for us to fit the curved walls. There is a table under one of the bookcases in the library which he made, and another long thin table, lacquered red, which goes behind the sofa and is usually covered with books. The walls here, above the panelled dado, are blue, and have a silk screen pattern in purple, making a sort of Gothic frieze above the level of the new bookshelves. This was designed by Ed Gilbert and Lucy Barlett who were then in partnership, and there again perhaps we were too cautious when it came to choosing the colours, because the purple only just shows up on the blue and in some lights you can hardly see it at all. On the other hand, I quite like that. The trouble with a house which has pretty architectural features is that you sometimes wonder if it wouldn't look best of all if you whitewashed the walls and left it empty.

All the rooms on the ground and first floors have three tall pointed windows, and we decided we didn't want to lose this shape by covering it with big curtains at night. Nor did it seem right to overpower a fairly small room with elaborate drapes over the tops of the windows. In the end we had the curtains cut to fit the arch, sewed them onto tape and tacked the tape onto the inside of the arch. The curtains are drawn by two strings running through rings at the top. We have used this design in all the rooms except those where we only have shutters.

Over the fire-place in the library we have an imaginary landscape by an eighteenth century painter called Richard Bampfylde. It belonged to my parents but turned out to be wholly appropriate for this part of the world, for Bampfylde was a West Country squire who was a friend of Henry Hoare of Stourhead, where there are a number of his pictures. Beneath it there is a little dark moonlight picture by John Crome the Younger which I bought in a sale in Bath some years ago. It needs cleaning. So does everything really. This was the first room we decorated when we came here twenty-two years ago, and it needs doing again. Whatever happened I should want it much the same; but that's because I dislike change rather than because I think it's perfect.

Isabel Colegate

Marian Brudenell

Deene Park
Northamptonshire

See O.S. Historic Houses p. 170

When I first visited Deene in January 1955 it was pathetically dilapidated and horribly uncomfortable.

There was a house party of twenty-four for a local dance and the warmth of the welcome from Mr. and Mrs. George Brudenell, my future father- and mother-in-law, obliterated the penetrating cold in the house. We were divided up into dormitories full of small iron beds with rocklike damp mattresses brought in from the stables. The sheets were grubby and I later discovered they were unwashed between visits but the top part ironed; the blankets had probably been at Balaclava and were crawling with maggots—it was like a ward at Scutari.

We were woken at dawn by the apparition of an ancient bandy-legged tramp who shambled into the room with logs to get the fire going. This proved not to be a ghost but Jo, who had started work here in 1903 and remained except for naval service in the First World War until his death in 1971.

Just as during the Civil War the house was plundered and extensively damaged by Cromwell's troops and needed restoration and refurnishing afterwards, so it was in 1945. Throughout the war the house was occupied by soldiers, British as well as Czechs, Poles and Indians, and by 1945 it had reached the nadir of decay. As Mr. and Mrs. Brudenell were quite unaware of decoration or of modern comforts it fell to my husband Edmund, while still in his teens, to persuade them to install electricity and some bathrooms. His father had held a three-day sale of the contents when he inherited in 1917 and more furniture was sold in 1948 to pay for installing electricity.

Deene is a large Elizabethan/Georgian house which has been home to thirteen generations of Brudenells and has reflected the changes in fortune of the family who over the centuries have enlarged, altered and patched it up so often. We wondered if we could ever manage to make it more habitable and continue to live in it and decided we couldn't bear to abandon it.

Deene Park.

We knew it would mean not only redecoration but extensive plumbing and electrical work, installing central heating and curing dry rot, not to mention buying furniture, carpets and curtains. The cost was inestimable and we would have to do it very slowly, just one room at a time and there were nearly a hundred!

My father- and mother-in-law (with whom we were to share the house for nearly seven years) gave us the Bow Room as our drawing-room and let us do it up how we liked. As it was the first of the eighty-six rooms we have done we particularly love it. It faces south with big French windows looking out to the garden and park and has bookcases on three walls, one of which is rounded with a fire-place in the centre. It had last been decorated in 1922, when the bookcases were painted iron grey and the walls a sickly yellowy beige. I was twenty-one, expecting twins and feeling rotten, and had no idea how to begin, so we con-

The oval drawing-room.

Lady Cardigan's brass four-poster is now back in her bedroom, together with prints and photographs of her and the hero of the Charge of the Light Brigade.

Part of the large drawing-room.

sulted Tony Howes who suggested that we should
avoid the sombre colours traditionally used in
libraries and take the softer colours from the Van
Dyck school portrait of the first Lady Cardigan
hanging over the chimney-piece. Coles made a
damask-patterned wallpaper in quite a strong,
rather dirty pink which admirably counteracts the
heaviness of the old leather bindings. The bookcases were painted white and we kept the old dull
brown plush curtains although we altered the deep
box-pleated pelmets. We bought comfortable
sofas and chairs to replace the old backbreakers
with horsehair seats and arranged them so that
people could talk to each other instead of shouting
across an open space.

We bought lamps with silk shades which give
a warmer light than the old barley-sugar standards
with dark parchment shades. Now, twenty-seven
years later, the room has changed a little. The Van
Dyck has been replaced by a Reynolds of a later
Lady Cardigan and we have improved the quality
of the furniture.

By 1948 the Victorian pale blue silk on the
drawing-room walls was rotten and hung down in
faded yellow festoons, but unfortunately it was
then replaced by a most dreary wallpaper. We
enlisted the help of Oliver Ford, who found a
lovely silvery blue American wallpaper reminis-
cent of the old silk and combined it with palest
blues, greens and yellows on chairs and carpet. It
is now a peaceful room dominated by the seventeenth century portraits. The furniture here is
mostly mediocre French—unfortunately good
French furniture was quite beyond us in price. We
were however very lucky to have started in the
fifties before prices went mad and when you could
still find bargains in back streets. We bought
masses of furniture, lots of china, usually chipped,
and rescued quite a few pictures of ancestors
which turned up in the salerooms.

It was great fun hunting things down and
rearranging the rooms for them. Finding the right
place is important but not always easy or obvious.
If everything in a room is all of the same date and
too carefully matched it has that clinical effect
frequently seen in museums and houses open to
the public. As Deene dates from Tudor to
Regency times with rooms of all sizes we have had
ample scope to avoid boredom, but we have always
considered what the original use and appearance
might have been and tried to use materials that are

Small ante-room full of pretty things.

either old or don't look glaringly new. Nothing has
been regilded and whenever possible things have
been repaired. Thank goodness we had a skilled
and cooperative house carpenter who became
adept at picture-hanging and altering panelling
and doors, and a team of willing hands who heaved
the furniture up and down and round about trying
to find where things looked best; we put picture
rails in every room so that pictures could hang
from chains and be moved without leaving the
walls scarred. Edmund used to get very irritated
by this 'earthquaking' and always wanted everything put back by dinner.

The most important room in the house is the
Elizabethan Great Hall with its hammerbeam
roof. It is very much the heart of the house and the

Left: *Seventeenth-century portraits hang on the silvery-blue walls of the peaceful drawing-room.*

Below: *Painting of the dining-room by John Sergeant, 1982.*

The dining-room today.

Country Life *photograph of The Great Hall, 1909.*

first room visitors see. In old photographs of 1909 and 1915 during the lifetime of the notorious Lady Cardigan it was an astonishing clutter of Victorian carved oak and leather chairs, oil lamps, stags' heads, mementoes of Balaclava and a whole stuffed tiger standing snarling menacingly on a gilt Queen Anne table. Above him on the oak panelling hung a magnificent Louis XIV clock which, together with the fire-place and the panelling from the other three walls, was sold in the twenties. The room degenerated into a barn, with brown silage paper on the walls and frosted glass replacing the seventeenth century stained glass in the windows. These were restored in 1959, and in 1963 the massive coarse fire-place dated 1571 was moved in from the billiard-room, the walls were plastered and painted, and the huge sofas with carved figures on the arms were brought back. Lady Cardigan, dressed in white satin even in her eighties, used to play the piano here and sing torrid love songs after dinner to the assembled, usually male,

company. She had been the adoring wife of the hero of the Charge of the Light Brigade whose junior she was by twenty-seven years. She died in 1915 after forty-seven years of merry widowhood at Deene only interrupted by a short-lived marriage to a Portuguese count. Her reputation was such that few ladies ever came here. Lady Cardigan was an accomplished, high-spirited woman, an excellent linguist and with a sharp wit, but her lively eccentricity shocked society. She wore Lord Cardigan's uniform trousers for bicycling, proposed marriage to Disraeli, wore thick white make-up and a blonde wig, had steeplechases over the gravestones in the churchyard and kept her coffin in the house, sometimes lying in it and asking how she looked! Some years ago her bed was offered back to us—my father-in-law had sold it in 1918—and of course we accepted with alacrity. It is a pretty brass four-poster and is now back in her bedroom covered in fine turquoise cotton. The room is full of prints and photographs of her and Lord Cardigan as well as a signed picture of the Pope, who rather surprisingly gave them an audience on their honeymoon. We used a Swiss wallpaper with a little all-over pattern and bought an old Scotch carpet in the perfect colours for two pounds ten at a sale.

Of all the Lady Cardigans Adeline must have been by far the most beautiful and amusing but her extravagance, with houses at Cowes, Newmarket, Melton and London as well as Deene and a yacht called the *Sea Horse*, led to the arrival of the bailiffs and the sale of her clothes, carriages and horses.

The bailiffs returned in 1928 and removed more things from the house, but luckily none of the family portraits without which the house would look depressingly bare. Though there are no great masterpieces they do give a valuable sense of continuity and are certainly decorative. We have had years of happiness and fun bringing the house back to life and pray that no disaster will cause the bailiffs to return or the contents to be dispersed again.

I hope that our descendants will live here and look after the old place and save it from the dreaded dead hand of a Committee or Institution.

Marian Brudenell

Barbara Cartland

CAMFIELD PLACE
Hatfield, Hertfordshire

In 1275 a knight called Camfield bought a few acres of ground near Hatfield in Hertfordshire and apparently retired there.

Later, in the reign of Queen Elizabeth I, a very beautiful Tudor manor house was built on the ground, with dovecots and fishpools as was customary in those days.

But the land had earlier been known to the Romans, and there is a Roman road going through the estate as well as a gravel-pit from which, from Roman days on, gravel was extracted for building.

In the eighteenth century Capability Brown was asked to landscape the park. It sloped down to a winding stream which eventually, after passing a great deal of woodland, reached the river Lea. This has now been enlarged to form two lakes.

In 1867 Edmund Potter, a rich industrialist from the North, pulled down most of the Tudor house and rebuilt Camfield Place. His granddaughter Beatrix Potter often stayed with him there, and in her biography there is a whole chapter written by her on 'The place I love best'. She undoubtedly wrote *The Tale of Peter Rabbit* about Camfield and illustrated some parts of her

'The most beautiful bed in the world'—a carved French four-poster dated 1650.

Above: *The library, containing over six thousand books, has deep blue panelling picked out in white.*
Below: *The kitchen forms an attractive setting for colourfully produced dishes.*

Favourite 'Egyptian' colours of Nile blue and bright coral pink are used in the bedroom.

grandfather's garden.

The door in the wall which the little rabbit couldn't squeeze underneath is still there, so is the goldfish pond where the white cat sat twitching his tail, and the potting-shed in which Peter Rabbit hid in a watering-can. In fact Mr. McGregor's garden is very much the same today as it is in her book.

In another part of the garden there is an oak tree planted by Queen Elizabeth I when she was a prisoner as a girl at Hatfield, to commemorate the spot where she shot her first stag. The acorns and leaves from this tree, which I have dipped in gold, are considered very lucky and people write from all over the world to tell me what benefits they have brought them.

The outside of the house is not very attractive, being late Victorian, but fortunately the inside was transformed by the previous owner, Lord Queenborough. He had two American millionairess wives, one of whom was the mother of Lady Baillie who owned the magnificent Leeds Castle. They put Georgian cornices in all the large, high rooms designed by Mr. Potter, added exquisite Adam mantelpieces, parquet flooring throughout the house and ten bathrooms. I have twelve, so there is no excuse for anybody to be dirty at Camfield Place.

What I have, which is unique and could not be found anywhere else, is a picture gallery which is actually a passage running right across the house; part of it belongs to the old Tudor manor, and it is entirely decorated with the original paintings done for the covers of my novels.

There must be over five hundred of these now. My first artist, Frances Marshall, whose designs have a special magic, is now unfortunately dead, but the work of two other artists decorates the walls and the only trouble is that I am beginning to run out of space!

During the war I altered the colouring of some of the most secret R.A.F. stations in England and it was proved that in doing so I improved morale. I am a tremendous believer in colour and my two favourites are Nile blue and bright coral pink, which I chose from the lovely Egyptian murals in the Valley of the Tombs of the Kings in Luxor. Wherever I have lived I have had these colours. While they are purely Egyptian in my bedroom, in the drawing-room the walls are a little more jade, as is the carpet, but the curtains are still a brilliant pink.

My library is to me one of the most important rooms in the house because it contains all the books that are absolutely essential to my work. For every novel I write I read twenty to thirty history books; it is very important that the background to every story should be correct as I am read in schools and universities all over the world. This room, which has a deep, almost peacock blue panelling picked out in white, contains over six thousand books. The carpet is a special shade of pink while the curtains and sofa are sunshine yellow.

Because I write between twenty and twenty-five books a year my secretaries' office is of paramount importance, and here again the walls are covered with some of the best and most beautiful of Frances Marshall's covers for my novels. The filing cabinets are all red, and so are the typewriters.

When my husband and I first came to Camfield Place in 1950 immediately after the war, there were heavy restrictions on how much decorating and improvements you could do. As Lord Queenborough died when he was eighty-eight, there was a great deal that wanted doing. I managed, however, to bring colour and beauty into every room and I collected the furniture I particularly love from antique shops for what seem now bargain prices.

One piece of furniture of which I am particularly proud and which is, in my opinion, the most beautiful bed in the world, I acquired in the most amusing manner.

I was motoring down from Scotland and stopped at Harrogate. I told somebody there that I wanted a four-poster bed and was informed there was one for sale in York. My son and I drove into York and I saw the shop I wanted to visit while we were stuck in a traffic jam. I left him, jumped out, went into the shop and saw an exquisite French four-poster dated 1650 which was beautifully carved. It had a sunburst of angels surrounding the Blessed Virgin over the bedhead. The original gilding was still on the canopy overhead, also the hook from which a lantern had been hung. I took one look, said I would have it, and ran back to my son.

The traffic jam was still outside so I took over the wheel of the car while he went into the shop, agreed it was exactly what we wanted, and was back in the car before the traffic had started to move.

I have had a great deal of the bed regilded and I myself, with plastic wood, mended the very few places on the canopy which needed it. There are two carvings of its original owner, one wearing his armour and the other his ordinary clothes. I feel because he was a Frenchman he would appreciate how much we all love and admire his bed.

It is always difficult to know what to do with caricatures. I shall never have as many as the Earl Mountbatten of Burma, who had half-a-dozen passages ornamented with his. But I have collected them all together and have them hung in the

The gentlemen's cloakroom houses an extensive collection of original Barbara Cartland caricatures.

gentlemen's cloakroom, where they amuse every guest who comes to the house. It seems a perfect place for them, and although it is not very easy I try whenever I am caricatured to buy the original from the artist.

As I am President of the National Association of Health, I believe good food is the foundation of good health. Therefore my kitchen is very important. It is, I think, beautiful; digestion starts with the eyes, and just as my dishes are lovely, many of them being a picture on the plate and as colourful and attractive as I can make them, so is where they are cooked. The wallpaper and the curtains are the design of the Bird of Paradise.

More than anything else what one needs in one's house is the right atmosphere, and when I came to Camfield Place I asked the local Rector who, fortunately, had lived in Jamaica so that he understood what was required, if he would bless my house. He blessed every room including the kitchen, which is most important, and I can confidently say that the house now has a lovely and peaceful atmosphere.

It was not until some years after we moved

here that Margaret Lane published the biography of Beatrix Potter and revealed that she had been frightened by ghosts in the hall and when she went up the stairs.

The only ghost we have now—and as I lived in a ghost house when I was a girl I dislike having them around me—is that of a black-and-white cocker spaniel which I had to have put to sleep because he had cancer.

I was the first person to see his ghost sitting under a table in the hall. My live dogs were frightened of him because at first he went for them ferociously when they tried to eat their dinner. Now he leaves them alone. Almost everybody in the house has seen him at some time or another.

He was a very sweet, quiet little dog and I think he stays with us because this was where he was happy and he does not wish to leave those he loved.

The garden is a bird sanctuary and the birds come every morning to eat the nuts which I put outside my bedroom window.

Apart from the pheasants we breed and my own free-range chickens, the estate is full of wildlife, even though we are only seventeen miles from London.

There are barking deer, foxes, squirrels, badgers and an inordinate amount of moles and, of course, we can never get rid of the 'Peter Rabbits'. Unfortunately they eat every flower I put in the garden with the exception of geraniums, and I therefore fill the flower-beds all around the house every year with bright coral pink geraniums, and hope the 'Peter Rabbits' will ignore them.

But they are, of course, part of Camfield Place and have 'owned' it for far longer than we have.

Diana Cooper

Little Venice, London

I think I will write about bedrooms, of which I have had quite a number in my long life. It is the room in most houses to which I'm the most attached—offering repose, sleep, privacy, or receiving of friends, clustered or singly, round a bed in which I weightless lie.

This is my life today and nearly every day and has been since I lost my independence— independence being my faithful little mini car, which I am too old to drive. Thus one comes back to one's beginning, but without independence or agility and with failing senses—consciously

worsening instead of the unconscious bettering from earliest childhood.

Like all my contemporaries, I spent two-thirds of my early life, together with a sister, in the night-nursery, the first unremembered in a small house in Bruton Street, still standing but now shop-fronted. (Once, many years ago, alone in my car, I followed a sirening fire engine quite a long way for fun, and found our flaming goal to be the house of my birth!)

In a little country house I suppose my family had taken for the five of us, there were curiously

Part of the drawing-room which has a very French atmosphere.

Lady Diana Cooper's present bedroom. The pale yellow french wall-paper is covered with small pictures.

A pretty arrangement of objects with a 'trompe l'oeil' in the background.

enough no country sports, so for my father, who enjoyed fishing, shooting, clubs, women and entertaining, there was nothing to do. At Hatley there were not even neighbours, no electric light or taps, or, of course, baths, only the silly tin slipper-shaped tubs in front of the fire-place.

We would often be taken to my grandfather's castle, called Belvoir, where life was much the same, no light or running water on the first floor, but watchmen indoors and out at night, who shouted most comfortingly. Every hour one would hear a gravelled footstep and then, 'Past twelve o'clock—all's well'.

Suddenly everything changed—a child died! Then, with Nanny and a governess for the older children, it was settled to expand in London, where a very beautiful enormous house, decorated by William Kent, was bought. We were all sad— change often saddens—a new night-nursery, habits unaltered—but, oh! the unexpected wonder of it! electric light and hot water you could turn on and off, and real long baths.

I spent more time in bed because I developed a muscular disease which lasted me three or four years. Stairs were forbidden, so my next bedroom was about as beautiful a reception-room as you could hope to find: mirrored walls, massively but delicately garlanded with chains of metal-gilded flowers. Here I slept with a criminal called 'Fraulein', only getting up at lunchtime and being carried to my mother's bed next door—another reception-room not half as gorgeous as mine, but both had two enormous windows looking onto Green Park where a military band played Gilbert and Sullivan once weekly. My mother's bedroom had a concealed proper bathroom, so we were complete.

Messenger boys, aged elevenish, took my mother's notes to her friends for sixpence and I went out all afternoon by hansom cab at half a crown an hour. In the mornings I had daily treatment, still in bed. The evening was pretty often the theatre, generally Shakespeare, including rehearsals at His Majesty's, the Beerbohm Tree family being interwoven with ours. I was cured by the age of eleven and lost my sensational reception bedsitter in disfavour of the schoolroom, looking onto a huge cobbled courtyard alive with cab and private horses stumbling away noisily.

Belvoir had become my father's, and my mother had decked it with light and water and I had my first real bedroom of my own—black-painted walls, a scooped alcove washing basin, self-painted to look as if under water, with a stone cockleshell (protruding) to hold the soap and swags of 'everlastings' in little bunches, and the narrowest, highest, reddest four-poster to the ceiling.

The whole arrangement was made more incongruous when I tell you that bang in the centre of the small, narrow room was a real punchball which I would punch by the hour in order to fight fat or to imagine I was chastising a lady I was not in favour of.

I was an adult at 14, making a bit of money by sewing a kind of chiffon 'top', to the knee, designed by the great Poiret (and lent me by a fashionable rich Parisian lady) and edged with silver braid, for three pounds, it costing me no more than fifteen shillings thank the Lord.

Another corner of Lady Diana Cooper's bedroom.

A brilliant few seasons in weekend 'stately homes'—two nights weekly in variable bedrooms—were followed by the utter change of Guy's Hospital, for the Great War was enforcing us all to work. I had a little room to myself, of which I was not master, for the essential light blazed you awake at 7 am and blacked you out at 10 pm, so I really have no memory of the room.

Peace, then marriage and looking for a house. I found one in a quarter of Bloomsbury, a quarter not yet the legend it became. It cost ninety pounds a year with Adam mantelpieces and the right window-panes—all-important to me, who could or would not live behind plate glass—and a charming garden with forest trees.

After a hundred identical bedrooms while theatrically touring America, my husband's career took us to Admiralty House. There was an outlook almost as sensational as the Green Park one, with a view of Whitehall and St. James's Park, and a bed held and rocked by golden dolphins, designed by Rex Whistler. Naturally I liked the bedroom best, though the ground floor was also crowded with

The small hall has silk on the walls.

golden dolphins. Downstairs was duty; my bedroom was bliss.

The next bedroom I remember was in Singapore in a charming little house deliberately built, except for the bedrooms, without doors or panes in windows. Again, in spite of the 'tick-tock' bird that hindered sleep, my refuge was my bedroom. The Japanese ousted us and so back to our Bognor home, sleeping to the lullaby of sea waves.

Peace was looming distantly and Algiers was our next mission—a new agony for me to be torn from happiest farming duties. There we found ourselves in a huge Arab house shared by another couple—Arctic cold in winter, no staff at all, washing at Harold Macmillan's next door, sleeping *in* my valuable mink coat. Yet it was still a joy to go upstairs to an agreeably proud bedroom.

Looking out of my window one spring morning I was surprised to see a semi-nude Arab crucified, with string, not nails, but frying in the violent sunshine, having been caught stealing. 'No', I was told, 'he can't be freed till midday.' So at midday he was brought down from his cross and left to return to his stealing.

The bedroom, as usual, became the club, with Randolph Churchill and Evelyn Waugh breakfasting on my bed; but still a refuge room.

Peace! And from peace to Paris as Ambassa-dor's wife. Panic! Everything that I most disliked, the only delight the most wonderful bedroom, said to have been Pauline Borghèse's (Napoleon's sister), repudiated, God knows why, by usual ambassadresses—probably because there was no bathroom, but I got one in a flash, fashioned like a tent in a space outside the door. The bedroom itself was sensational—walls, curtains, screens, sofas and chairs all of the same crimson red silk and a vast bed of the same silk crowned at all but ceiling height by an imperial eagle and supported by *retour d'Egypte* figures. A few of the chairs' seats were beginning to wear, and I suggested to what was then called the Office of Works that they order a hundred metres of the identical silk to be kept for future dilapidation at the Embassy. My surprise was total upon discovering that the identical material came not from Lyons but from Macclesfield, England.

After two or three years in the country's service, wearying, but restored by the bed, we moved out of Paris to a very pretty little house within the walls of the park of Chantilly, where from my bedroom I looked south onto well-tended grass sloping down to an important lake, fed by an even more important cascade. No traffic, no tourists—only woodland groves, peopled by beautiful silent statues.

I came home after about ten years, alas! alone, and found myself a house I would exchange with no other in the best of all quarters—Little Venice—whose bedroom, whence I scribble now, I still find the room of the rooms in the house I like best, with forest trees in the garden, a big bed and tiny dog—still, and as always, a *refuge*.

Diana Cooper

The Duchess's four-poster bed has an arched cornice and painted fluted posts. The chintz bed hangings match the window curtains.

Deborah Devonshire

CHATSWORTH
Bakewell, Derbyshire

If you are a woman who finds herself married to the hereditary owner of what used to be known as a stately home and is now called a historic house, you soon become aware of the unwritten rules of primogeniture.

You live in furnished rooms, surrounded by things which do not and never will belong to you. You are also aware that if you should become a widow you move, pronto, and the familiar things stay.

All interest is centred on the eldest son and his family. Younger sons are looked on as a sort of long-stop insurance but the birth of a daughter is greeted with sighs from the family solicitor. This situation is taken for granted by Englishwomen. It is the way of primogeniture and it is the reason that, in spite of savage taxation, there are still wonderful interiors in English houses, hundreds of which can be seen by paying a pound or two in the season. I have seen it from both sides, having married a younger son who became his father's heir through the depredations of war. It is part of the Great Unfairness of Life, but it works.

At Chatsworth there is ample evidence of the

Looking to the fire-place of the small sitting-room. The walls are hung with dark green watered silk.

system. Furniture and pictures from abandoned Cavendish houses (Devonshire House and Chiswick House in London, Compton Place at Eastbourne and Hardwick Hall in Derbyshire) crowd the attics and give so much to choose from that, as well as rearranging most of the rooms here, I have furnished two country hotels.

In 1957 we began to think about moving back into Chatsworth. The family had left in 1939 and a girls' school moved in with the war—three hundred girls and their teachers lived there in discomfort till 1946, sleeping in passages and state rooms and doing their lessons in any suitable space. After that the house was empty. My mother-in-law made the huge effort to get it reopened for people to see round in 1949 and the staff of ten Hungarians she engaged did magnificent work cleaning and making ready the rooms on the public route round the house. They did not have time to do much to the rest and it was very depressing to come over from our own house in the village a mile away and look at the shuttered rooms, so shabby and having that special stale, closed-up smell.

When we decided to come and live here we considered which bit of the house we would use. There are a hundred and seventy-five rooms at the last count so the possibilities were endless but we soon settled for the traditional rooms used by the family. These are on the first floor facing south and west. We have never regretted it.

Work went on for nearly two years. We put in seventeen bathrooms and central heating. (Till 1939 there was one bath and lavatory for seven visitors' bedrooms on the east side of the house.) This meant water going long distances to rooms which it had not reached before. Slowly the smell of emptiness and decay gave way to the smell of paint and now it is only by an effort that I can remember how squalid and dingy the rooms were after being shut up for years.

Because of the shape (and size) of this house it is wonderfully convenient to live in when it is open in the summer. The people who come to see round go straight from the ground floor to the second floor where the state rooms are. You can sit in the drawing-room on the first floor and be unaware that a thousand other people are in the house at the same time. So well built is it that the faintest murmur, like a distant sea, is all you hear.

I was lucky when I started work on the house

A mixture of old and new pictures against the slub silk walls of the bedroom.

in 1958 because Andrew gave me a free hand so I only had to please myself. I think the role of a professional decorator must be very difficult. He has to please his client and can rarely do just what he wants, but when the job is finished his name is connected with it however much he may regret the decisions of the client. I can't imagine employing a decorator, partly because I am too mean but mostly because I love looking for the materials and other necessities myself. It is like hunting, and is nearly as exciting when, after drawing blank for days, you suddenly find the stuff you want.

Because of the vast size of the house (the roof is one and a third acres) I will try and describe the two rooms I spend most time in, or I shall overrun my allotted space by thousands of words.

In 1958 the Duchess's bedroom still had a peeling blue wallpaper left from the 1930s and the doors and paintwork were of the dreariest, dirtiest buff. The four-poster bed was so shrouded in dustsheets (and dust) that you could not guess what it was like. It had been a classroom during the war but the bed was left as there was nowhere else to put it.

When we unpacked the bed it revealed an arched cornice painted with flowers and painted fluted posts. We found the bed hangings, which match the window curtains. They are made of a chintz with bunches of flowers as 'filling' and wide borders of huge peonies and chrysanthemums, a pattern which is repeated in other bedrooms in the house. I have never seen it anywhere else. It is strikingly beautiful and is of Chatsworth scale and quality. The silk-covered bobbles are just a row of wooden pegs now with traces of the old silk clinging to them. I got new lining for the canopy and curtains, blue jap silk from John Lewis, clean and cheap.

The walls are covered with pale blue slub silk bordered by a gilt fillet of a complicated pattern. Nearly all the bedrooms have these fillets in different designs. John Fowler told me they are made of *papier maché* on wire and that they are Italian.

The sofa at the foot of the bed has never been covered (laziness) but is wrapped in one of those old white cotton bedspreads with patterns made of bubbles of air. I wish I knew where to get this stuff. Perhaps it doesn't exist any more.

Three large dogs share the room with me and my sister Diana says it has a zoo smell. One of them likes sleeping under the bed and does something awful to the springs when he turns over.

The ornaments all seem to be to do with chickens. The best are a pair of Belgian faience hens, with eggs attached and chicks on their backs and under their wings.

In 1941 my aunt gave me three pounds to buy myself a wedding present. I rushed to Peter Jones and got the triple mirror which is on the dressing table.

The pictures are a mixture of old and new, Landseer, Epstein, Allingham, Duncan Grant, Millet, Rosa Bonheur, two Helleus of my mother, and various unknowns. The latest acquisition is some Huggins poultry.

I wake up very early and make my breakfast here. The strident colours of the electric kettle and toasting machine are a blot on the landscape but the comfort of not having to wait for a civilised hour outweighs that. I try not to have it before seven but I can see the time coming when it will be six and then five. It is early in the morning when all is quiet that I look around and realise how lucky I am to sleep in such a room.

The little sitting-room nearby is a complete change from the high drawing-rooms. In the last century a floor was put in so it is half the original height, and gives a mezzanine above. I am glad this was done because it makes the sitting-room of more human scale and the space above is a precious one for hanging clothes, hiding Christmas presents and keeping the mass of things acquired over the years.

There were dingy beige cotton hangings on the wall, a relic of Granny and years ago. It was the headmistress's study while the school was here.

I got dark green watered silk from George Spencer of Sloane Street and they hung it. It is box-pleated every four inches and fixed by a plain gilt fillet I found in the stable loft. After twenty-five years it has faded a bit but there is no harm in that and you only notice it when a picture is moved. The floor is covered in beige felt, which seems better than plain pile where a pattern might be too muddling to the eye. By the fire is a needlework rug with snakes sewn into it.

The paint below the dado, and the ceiling, is dead white; unfashionable, but it is what I like. Most of the furniture came from Compton Place at Eastbourne. It is smaller in scale than the native Chatsworth things and extremely pretty and pleasant to live with.

The sofa and armchair are covered in cotton with a dark green oak-leaf design. The covers are worn out and the piping cord hangs loose from the cushions. You can still get the stuff in any colour except the one I like, which is a warning to buy twice as much as you want in the first place. Extravagant I know, but as Hamish Erskine used to say when he took a taxi instead of a bus for fear of getting lost, it's cheaper in the end.

The writing table is an inlaid English beauty made by Ince and Mayhew, who supplied furniture for the drawing-rooms here in 1786. It is so smothered in letters and ornaments and flowers that I have resorted to spikes to hold papers which really must not be lost. Sometimes I find the bottom letters have answered themselves by being there for so long and with great satisfaction I throw them away.

There are swatches of patterns, architects' plans, more and more writing paper, photographs waiting to be stuck into albums, reference books, farm reports, files, ponies' pedigrees, half-written speeches, lists for tomorrow, and other signs of

Corner of the sitting-room. The inlaid writing-table was made by Ince and Mayhew, who supplied furniture for the Chatsworth drawing-rooms in 1786.

extra-mural activities on the floor. I spend a great deal of time looking for things I have lost and I beg people not to leave an important paper near my room without keeping a copy. On a windowsill is every one of the magazine *Interiors* since it started. The pile is beginning to topple now.

I am no good at indoor flowers and can't do arrangements so I plump for plants in pots, preferably the kind that last a long time. There is a glorious portrait of a woman by Velasquez which I can see from the writing table. The lower half of her is usually obliterated by flowers.

I think all pictures look well on the green silk. There is a strange mixture in this little room. An early Freud, a tiny Millais watercolour, a Boldini drawing of my mother's foot, a Turner of Oxford of sheep on Salisbury plain with Stonehenge in the background, some framed ivory and wax pictures,

a Landseer portrait of the sixth Duke in his box at the opera, the fourth Duke's children in the garden at Chiswick by Zoffany, some Crawhall chickens, Wootton racehorses and Barden Tower by Atkinson Grimshaw. To look at such a mixture every day is pure pleasure.

Books are a bother. They grow in number in the most extraordinary way. I'm all for a bookcase full of books (and there are two such in here, one a blocked-up door which someone put shelves in), but when they fall about all over the place what are you to do? It seems awful to throw them away when you think of what a trouble they are to write. Perhaps I will put a second-hand book stall in the shop.

There are two big boxes where I throw letters from family and friends. I suppose few people write to each other as often as we all do and the quantities are a bit daunting, but I couldn't bear to tear them up.

I feel sorry for the person who has to clear out this room when I have gone. It is encrusted with *things*. It is like the room in Ireland described by Somerville and Ross when they were trying to pack up before moving . . . 'Under *everything* there is *something*'.

The view from this side of the house is one of the joys of living here. Below is the West Garden, with its plan of Chiswick House in golden box. You look over it to the river Derwent and James Paine's three-arched bridge beyond, then a mile or more of close-cropped grass and huge trees and up the hill to the high woods on the distant skyline.

If ever I have a house of my own I will try something different, partly because nothing could be as beautiful as Chatsworth and partly because I should not want to embark on rooms and furniture which have to be looked after.

I expect it will have blockbusting heating, painted floors, office furniture made of tin, filing cabinets with drawers which open and shut with terrifying ease, a shiny red writing table from Rymans and an Executive Chair with a swivel seat covered in beige tweed. The cabinets will be empty because I will have nothing to do. It will feel very odd.

Deborah Devonshire

Daphne Fielding

The Laundry
Badminton, Avon

Like Mrs. Tiggywinkle of Beatrix Potter fame, I live in a laundry—the old laundry of Badminton House, owned by the Duke of Beaufort. It was built in 1662—a sundial marks this date. The classical Caroline building stands alone beside a large reach of water which used to be known as 'the horse-pond' and is contained by sunken drystone walling. Here, in what is now my home, the laundry of a succession of dukes and duchesses, their families and visitors was washed, blue-bagged, starched, ironed and goffered.

When I first saw where I was going to live, the

laundry had not functioned as such for many a year and had become a mere shell—a beautiful grey fossilised shell. Inside, the ceiling was falling down, walls were crumbling, and below an eczema of flaking plaster the old narrow red bricks showed. Rats had invaded. There were still broken remains of wooden drying screens that used to be manipulated by rope-pulleys and hung with bedlinen and household napery after it had been washed, scrubbed and boiled in a great copper. Brick niches, like old-fashioned bakers' ovens, were built into the walls for the heating of

Looking across and out of the living-room.

flat-irons on red-hot embers. On the far side of the water, clothes-lines were set in an orchard of apple trees.

The horse-pond has now become a crowded duck-pond inhabited by descendants of the white 'Call ducks' brought there by Mary Cambridge when she married the last duke in 1923.

Wild mallard ducks from other waters fly in at dusk. Some of these foreigners have become squatters. They are a rough lot and molest the white Jemima Puddleducks which have crossed with Aylesburys, resulting in a strain peculiar to this pond and which increases yearly despite nocturnal raids of foxes — lords of the animal world at Badminton. But . . . back to square one and how I came to live here.

My son-in-law, David Somerset, is the present Duke. The restoration of the laundry was his project, and he asked that brilliant architect Philip Jebb (Hilaire Belloc's grandson) to submit a plan on which they worked closely together.

I had been living in France for fifteen years and wanted to return to England, when out of the blue came the wonderful offer of the laundry — to come and live there when the restoration was finished and make it my permanent home. I could hardly believe my good fortune.

Philip Jebb's blueprint was to feature one very big room and I was asked whether I would prefer a large bedroom or living-room. Without hesitation I plumped for a big living-room; I like a womb-pocket of a bedroom (with room to swing a Pekingese) and a rather larger bathroom which I can also use as my dressing-room. When the work was nearly finished I moved from France and stayed with my daughter and son-in-law in their house at the gates of the park. While I was staying with them I visited the site most days, clutching Jebb's blueprint which began to crack at the folds. I also made many trips to Bath and London to get patterns of wallpapers and snippets of fabric for curtains, furniture upholstery and loose covers.

I was positive that I wanted the big room to be cream and white. My friend Alan Tagg — one of the best of our stage decorators — told me of a paint he had often used successfully; its colour name is 'Buttermilk'. This has a pinkish glow coming through pale cream; it is lovely.

Furniture removers from England bringing a friend's furniture out to France returned with the empty van crammed full with all my treasures;

Corner of the drawing-room.

none of great value, but infinitely precious to me because I am a sentimental magpie. The provenance of most of my furniture and objects springs from two grandmothers and the *salle des ventes* at Nîmes. All arrived safely at Badminton but when unloaded most of them seemed unworthy of the noble big room which forms the heart of the house. This is almost a double cube but, like all the rooms in Badminton, proved slightly uneven when it came to taking measurements; this, I think, adds a certain charm. It has four double mullion windows with the original lead surrounding the square panes and a French window-cum-door. The ceiling is very high and has a fine cornice — the copy of one in my son-in-law's house in the village; a plastercast was taken from the original.

The windows at the far end of the room have window seats in recesses contained by the thick walls. From these I can observe the duck-pond. The French window on the opposite side of the room leads into a cobbled courtyard where a short roofed-in passage is the approach to my front door; through it a sweep of grass lawn, the big house and another world.

The cobbled courtyard is very French in feeling and viewed through the front door gives one the impression that it will lead to a *pavillon de*

The Old Laundry, with Badminton House behind.

chasse. Before the restoration it was covered by a glass roof and strips of corrugated iron. When I first saw it a lone lavatory stood against a wall and still flushed; its make was 'Niagara'!

The big room has lovely details. In a store-room at Badminton House a beautiful Kent chimney-piece languished unseen. Kent was the architect of the house and this must be contemporary. The last Duke in his great kindness let me have it installed in my big room. It is my favourite thing there. In the centre set between wreaths of fruit and flowers is a head of Diana, goddess of the chase, with a crescent moon in her hair. Swags of full-blown roses and plums hang from two stylised pedestals on either side. There is a Greek key pattern border below the shelf they support. Here I have green glass obelisks and two Jean Petiot figures of a sultan and sultana. Rising above it is a big Regency mirror.

I had borrowed an elegant Georgian fire-basket which stood on legs. It was in keeping with the Kent mantelpiece but eighty per cent of the heat of the fire was lost up the chimney, so I am installing a Norwegian cast-iron stove copied from a classical American colonial design. Either side of it will stand two andirons—cast-iron figures of autumn and winter which marry well with the mantelpiece. I bought these at an auction sale in Nîmes.

Some people are totally unable to visualise the restoration and conversion of a building with prophetic eyes. Many of my friends who saw the laundry in its state of ruin were convinced that the big room would be dark. In point of fact, it is dancing with light which, on a sunny day, reflects off the water onto the ceiling.

My curtains are full and long with deep pel-mets. They are interlined with padding and the material is chintz. The design, rather like Chinese wallpaper, has big pink peonies, fuchsia and yellow lilies on a cream-coloured ground. They were made by Yvonne Nettles, the daughter-in-law of the housekeeper at Badminton. Her husband did the carpentry required for this job. All my curtains and pelmets have been made with a *tête flamande* (French heading). I love this because it looks like smocking and reminds me of children's frocks.

The big room leads into the kitchen, which has two views. My back door opens onto the 'waterfront' and a French window onto the cob-bled courtyard with its pot plants and window-boxes. It is 'wood fitted' and the colour of a hazel nut. Tiles surround the gas oven range, grill and 'washing-up department'. On the walls I have a Coles wallpaper with a small design of intertwining flowers. The roller blinds are made in a matching fabric and I have a brown Frigidaire. The floor is covered with linoleum which fakes Provençal tiles. I rather wish I had used big cork tiles.

Big prints of fruit which belonged to my grandmother look well here. I have had them in the dining-room of every house I have lived in.

When I first saw Jebb's plan I was most of all delighted by the fact that it showed me I would be able to go straight out of my bedroom and make myself a cup of tea at 6.30 am when my alarm clock rings. This is the time of day that I like best—when the telephone does not torment and nothing disturbs.

My tiny bedroom had the ceiling lowered, as did the kitchen, to keep the heat in. Here I have a Coles wallpaper with matching material which hangs from below the cornice to the floor. The design has prim little bunches of pink lilies of the valley on an ivory-coloured ground. My bed faces onto the pond and again there is a window seat with heating installed below. This is very effective and unobtrusive. It looks like picket fencing—'pretty maids all in a row' style.

My primrose-coloured bathroom is the best I have ever known. It is just opposite my bedroom, a few steps across a little lobby with a window. From this and the bathroom there is yet another view onto a green lawn, the old malt-house where beer used to be brewed and a part of the stables. I can look out of these windows and tell which way the wind is blowing from the weather-vane over the stables—a running fox.

The bath is huge, panelled in wood stained mahogany colour and varnished. The carpentry was executed by a local craftsman. This bathroom reminds me of one in an old-fashioned yacht or liner. I particularly like the lights over the looking-glass and the washing basin (called by the plumber the 'toilet unit' and all enclosed in wood, like the bath). These bracket wall-lights have jointed arms. They are made of brass and designed by Billy Baldwin. I have a collection of Victorian shell pictures in octagonal frames above the bath.

A theme of trellis and basket patterns runs through this little house. It recurs on the floor of the big room in the design of the Portuguese rugs. Baskets are everywhere, and happily there is a wonderful weaver at nearby Acton Turville who made me a huge square log basket for firewood.

One of the things I like best about the laundry

The primrose-coloured bathroom has a huge, wood-panelled bath, stained mahogany. Above the bath is a collection of Victorian shell pictures.

is the vistas Jebb's plan provided. With one room leading into another, looking through, I am often reminded of a Dutch picture. Perhaps above all I love the pond views from my window seats. In the spring there are yellow ducklings and moorhen chicks which take to the water as soon as they are hatched and look like black fluffy walnuts. A lone grey heron stands like the ghost of a statue waiting for fish. The pond is stocked with ancient and enormous carp which jump out of the water before an electric storm. No one is allowed to fish for them. I am particularly fond of the view onto the opposite side of the pond. The big willows leaning against each other might well have been painted by Corot.

My need is to live close by water. I have been drawn to pond life ever since I brought tadpoles back from Le Touquet in a jam-jar when I was twelve. *The Wind in the Willows* was my first favourite book. It is by my bedside here—the edition with the Shepard illustrations.

One day a rather affected art dealer was lunching with my son-in-law and I was sitting next to him. 'Tell me', he said, 'when you are in residence in your laundry, will you dress as Marie Antoinette did at Le Petit Hameau? Perhaps like a laundress painted by Madame Vigée Le Brun?' Such an idea ruffled me.

'Certainly not', I replied. 'I'll probably be dressed like Toad of Toad Hall when he was on the run in drag, disguised as a washerwoman with that little black bonnet tied under his chin.'

Waking up each morning is an adventure here. I've never paddled my own canoe before and it is a challenge.

I share my pond life with two familiars. A green Amazon parrot who behaves like the geese of Troy, giving warning when anyone approaches and capable of making noises like a pack of bloodhounds, and a young Pekingese who is rather too fascinated by the duck.

The kitchen, looking onto the 'waterfront'.

Christina Foyle

BEELEIGH ABBEY
Maldon, Essex

My lovely home, Beeleigh Abbey, lies surrounded by twelve acres of gardens on the banks of the river Chelmer. It is a Premonstratensian abbey, built in the latter part of the twelfth century, and it remains in a surprisingly perfect state of preservation. A Tudor timber-framed wing was added soon after the Dissolution, in about 1560. For hundreds of years the place lay neglected, a home for farmers, with the largest room housing their sheep and cows. Then in 1911 Colonel Grantham bought it and beautifully restored it, making it a lovely comfortable

home without in the least disturbing the peaceful tranquillity, the legacy of the monks. It is a fairytale place with a romantic history, all of it happy. The monks wore white habits and they bore romantic names—Andreln, living here in 1265, William de Rokelaunde in 1320, Richard de Purlee in 1384. One of the monks knew and corresponded with Peter Abelard. The most loved was a merry monk who is immortalised in the fresco painting of a cock in the monks' warming-room, a reminder that there was lighthearted fun in this religious community.

One of the bedrooms with seventeenth-century four-poster.

The patrons too fire the imagination—Henry Bourchier, first Earl of Essex, who was buried here, Isobel, Countess of Essex, sister of Richard, Duke of York, the father of Edward IV who, with his queen, visited the Abbey. We have their portraits in the calefactory, which is the main room. It was the monks' dining-room and we use it as our sitting-room. Its superb vaulted roof is supported by a row of pillars made of Purbeck marble brought in by barge from the West Country eight centuries ago. The huge fire-place is surrounded by a carved stone frieze of six angels, part of the canopy of the tomb of the Abbey's patron Henry Bourchier, Earl of Essex.

All through the winter, and often through the English summer, we have a huge log fire burning. There is a constant supply of logs from our surrounding woodland. The furniture is very comfortable—a big soft sofa, deep armchairs, Oriental rugs laid on rush matting to soften the original monastic austerity, and masses of flowers from the garden and greenhouse.

When we have guests, we entertain in this room. There is a magnificent oak refectory table about fourteen feet long made from two perfect planks of wood from the same enormous tree. Twenty people can be comfortably seated at this table.

We are lucky to have traced the original stained-glass windows from Beeleigh. They had been stored for many years in Westminster Abbey. The windows depict the life of the Virgin Mary and they are now in their original place.

Some of my favourite pictures are in this room. Among them is the portrait of Baretti, great friend of Dr. Johnson and Fanny Burney and also the compiler of a famous dictionary. There is a lovely court scene of fair ladies by Matania, one of my favourite artists, and two wonderful moonlight scenes by Pether Senior. The pictures look very dark, with just the full moon shining, but if a light is shone on them wonderful little figures, woodmen sitting by their fires with their animals, a castle almost hidden in the trees, a lamp shining through the latticed window of a cottage, fishermen preparing their boat for the morning, all emerge from the shadows.

The whole Abbey is so lovely that the less furniture the better. My father's contribution and legacy was the wonderful library. Perhaps mine has been the pictures, a very personal collection. I have been fortunate all my life in knowing artists and many have given me pictures. My favourites are those by the painters of fairy tales, Edmund Dulac and Arthur Rackham. Sir Alfred Munnings gave me a delightful self-portrait and Sir Gerald Kelly a typical charming painting of a Burmese dancing girl. This hangs in my bedroom. Many artists, Doris Zinkeisen, Kitty Shannon, relation of Shannon and Ricketts of legendary fame, and the brilliant Zsuzsi Roboz have painted portraits of me and these are hung discreetly about the place. I love children's books and their illustrators

Christina Foyle's bedroom showing a corner of her four-poster bed.

and have an enchanting collection of Kate Greenaway and Ernest Shepherd originals.

When I find an artist specially appealing, I ask him to paint the Abbey. Nicholas Ridley has recently painted an exquisite picture in his own romantic style, and Felix Kelly, whose work so much resembles that of Rex Whistler, has added to my collection.

We have an art gallery in Foyles where artists and craftsmen exhibit. All kinds of work are shown, embroidery, jewellery, engraved glass, pottery, and from every exhibition I buy something lovely to embellish the Abbey.

Beyond the calefactory is a private chapel used for family weddings and christenings. To reach the chapel, you go through a small anteroom whose use was explained to me by Mr. Enoch Powell. It was where visitors to the monks

Small, heavily timbered drawing-room.

Another corner of the calefactory room.

The Monks' dormitory now housing Christina Foyle's father's collection of books and manuscripts.

🐚 *The calefactory now the main sitting-room with a fine vaulted ceiling.*

used to be put up and was called 'The Slype'. We had always used it as a larder, but when the shelves became rather shabby we had the cupboard stripped out, and there were revealed original wall paintings done by the monks.

We made this place into a delightful small dining-room as it is near the kitchen. There are a circular marble table and very pretty oak chairs with blue velvet cushions. It is here that we have the Felix Kelly picture of the Abbey. Local craftsmen who specialise in church restoration helped me. There was a very small bricked-in window; they enlarged this and built a Gothic frame based on the original design of the Abbey windows and I commissioned John Hayward, whose beautiful stained glass I had admired at the Goldsmith's Hall, to design a window giving the whole history of the Abbey. The result is superb, and one of the most attractive features of our home. Everything is in it, in glowing colours—the early monks in their habits, the canonised St. Roger, King Edward and Queen Eleanor, Henry VIII and his evil friend Sir John Gate, to whom he bestowed the Abbey and who was later executed on Tower Hill, my father's library, and even the sheep and cows which once lived in the main room. A scroll in the corner lists the distinguished visitors to the Abbey. This will make interesting reading in a hundred years' time. How I wish that the monks

An outside view of Beeleigh Abbey.

had left a similar record.

In the chapel, stone plaques list the names of the monks, patrons and secular owners. There is an interesting organ which came from the Foundling Hospital and was actually built in the old organ loft in Manette Street off Charing Cross Road, the home of Foyles. Handel once played on this organ.

The vicar holds services in the chapel on summer Sundays and it is a lovely English scene, with families picnicking on the lawn and the sound of hymns on the evening air.

From the other end of the calefactory steps lead to the Tudor Wing, a charming small drawing-room, heavily timbered, with a splendid open fire-place. French windows open onto a sunken garden with a goldfish pool, and from mid-morning until evening on a summer day this room is bathed in sunshine. The décor, carpets, sofa and chairs are pale pink, giving the room an extra glow. The pictures, a Matania and a Conder fan, blend delightfully with the surroundings.

Above the calefactory is the monks' dormitory, now our library, housing my father's collection of manuscripts and rare books. The room is quite breathtaking in its beauty, with its great roof of chestnut timbers, its early sixteenth century windows looking out over the Essex marshes, and its magnificent library of exquisite bindings. Here hangs the portrait of my father by Dugdale and the enigmatic Chandos portrait of Shakespeare.

This room, indeed the whole house, is so beautiful that very little furniture or decoration is needed. If a room gets shabby and the hangings and carpets show signs of wear, I seek the help of artists. Henry Bardon, who designs the lovely scenery for the Covent Garden ballets and for Glyndebourne, has made a bedroom into a fairytale world of fantasy. He has painted frescoes of poetic scenes—forest glades, winding rivers, hidden away castles and, in the connecting bathroom, gorgeous birds. There is a coal fire and the most comfortable sofa and chairs, the colours of the upholstery blending with the paintings on the walls. The bed is a four-poster made in 1613, and the bedspread was woven by one of the artists who exhibited in my gallery. I found the perfect picture for the room, a wild woodland scene by de Loutherbourg, also a stage artist painting for the theatre in about 1800. To wake up in this room is an aesthetic experience.

In all there are seven bedrooms, four with their own bathrooms, and the beds are Tudor carved four-posters—very attractive and comfortable.

One magnificent bed was built for James I, and in this room we have a collection of books connected with the monarch. These include several very beautiful bindings with the royal arms embossed and most of the books written by James I, who was a considerable author, including his famous diatribe against tobacco.

There is a charming small suite of rooms at the far end of the library which we use for guests. One is a music room with a piano and records and everything to make a visitor happy.

An enormous loft runs the whole length of the building. It was here that my father kept a model railway of steam and electric trains, stations, terminals—everything to delight the heart of an enthusiast. My father and the vicar spent many happy hours here together, and when my father died I gave the whole set to the vicar who was quite overwhelmed. The loft now houses Foyles Anti-

A postcard dated 1903 picturing Beeleigh Abbey.

quarian Book Department.

The Abbey really is one of the loveliest homes in England. Every room is beautiful and the prospect from each window gives delight. Some look over lawns where peacocks strut, others to the river and the marshes, but everywhere it is peaceful and serene. Although so remote, the place is not lonely. Students often stay to study the manuscripts, and book collectors come from all over the world to look at our treasures.

We have cared for Beeleigh Abbey for more than forty years, looking upon it as a sacred trust, and it is my dearest wish that whoever follows us here will feel as we do about this lovely and hallowed place.

Christina Foyle

Diana Gage

THE HOLE OF ELLEL
Cark-in-Cartmel, Grange-over-Sands, Cumbria

The old ordnance maps mark the Hole of Ellel in gothic letters signifying a site of archaeological interest. The Lancashire County Record Department at Preston have no information, so perhaps it was a myth. When we were making an approach to the house, the pickaxe struck a large stone which rang hollow. Hoping for an exciting discovery I dug much deeper than necessary, only to locate an early land drain.

The late Steven Potter who wrote about English place names thought the name Hole of Ellel derived from a Norse invader and was 'Ella's Nook'—'Who and what was Ella you must find out' he said, but no one seems to know. The rest of the address describes the surrounding country.

There may have been an early habitation here. It is sheltered from the north and east, on rising ground, and there was a nearby stream, now part of an underground reservoir.

In the seventeenth century it was recorded that Mrs. Preston from Holker retired to the dower house at Ellel. There are lumps in the field that may have been buildings, so it is possible; though there is another Ellel near Lancaster.

The original back door is now the main entrance. The flooring is half-polished, blue-grey slates.

The Hole of Ellel stands on rising ground and faces south-west. The main part probably dates from the eighteenth century.

The main part of the house as it is now probably dates from the eighteenth century. It was originally a square simple farmhouse; the part to the east was built on at the beginning of this century and combined to make two cottages. It is near my childhood home, and when young we always thought it delightful. Facing south west, across fields and woods, it gives just a glimpse of cottage roofs and the sands and tides of Morecambe Bay over to the far shore of the Furness Peninsula.

I first came to live here as a widow in 1946.

Another part of the sitting-room has charming water colours by Ian Campbell-Gray.

The long, blue-green sitting-room has a fire-place either end.

The main part of the house was inhabited by a grand old lady, Mrs. Fox, who had been there most of her life, so I had the bit on the east side. This consisted of kitchen to the north, sitting-room opposite, to the south. Upstairs two bedrooms and a bathroom.

The kitchen had a small open fire with an oven attached, a grate with cast-iron daffodils. This also heated the water. It was warm and looked quite welcoming but cooking was difficult. Later a dual-purpose cooker was installed. More practical, but the prevailing wind from the west made the cooker roar and shake the house like a liner under stress in a storm. We ate in the kitchen

A drawing by the Viscountess Gage's sister, Mary Countess of Crowford, done in 1946, representing Mrs. Fox who originally lived in the main part of the house.

but guests said they preferred the simpler, old-fashioned atmosphere. Later I had calor gas.

The sitting-room had a good-sized window, bookcases built into two walls and an open wood-burning fire-place. Everywhere painted white. I had lived in a small house in London and the furniture was just right for size here. This room is now a dining-room.

I kept a little visitors' book, and looking back am astonished at the kindness of friends who braved an extremely simple life and came to stay.

In 1947 the other part of the house became available, so it was possible to make it one. Ways through were made on the ground and upper floors. The old walls were three feet thick and consisted of very large boulders filled in with smaller undressed stones.

Central heating was a primary consideration and for months workmen, mostly local, were installing pipes, rendering walls, plastering, painting.

The levels of the two parts of the house are

different, so regretfully the staircase from the east side had to be removed.

The back door to the north opened directly into the kitchen but I made it into the main entrance with a little hall. For flooring the Burlington quarries across the Bay provided beautiful blue-grey slates cut two and a quarter feet square and half polished, which makes them nearly black and gives a good surface.

The remaining staircase is on the north side and direct from the hall, with a long window which goes the length of the house. Very typical of the north country—and there is a window in the garden door to the east so quite a lot of crosslight.

A cupboard door under the stairs opens onto a steep stair down to a cellar which still has the original hooks in the ceiling for hanging hams, and rough slate slabs. It is ideal for storage. For a time I had a smallholding, Jersey cows, Tamworth pigs, Rhode Island Red chickens, an orchard and bees, and the cellar fulfilled a much-felt need. The kitchen sheltered some bereaved piglets for a short time.

The living-room faces south west onto a little terrace. It consisted of two little rooms divided by a passage with what was once a front door. I took away one of the walls but it was not right; so later removed both walls, making a longish sitting-room with a fire-place either end. The garden door is in the middle, its top half glazed, and there are windows with acid yellow curtains either side. The room is painted bluey-green. One wall is books. The pictures, as in most of the other rooms in the house, are by my husband Ian Campbell-Gray.

Finance was always a problem, but luckily the curtains and carpets as well as the furniture from London fitted in all right and have not been replaced until absolutely in tatters. Similarly, when I made a sitting-out place to the west of the sitting-room terrace, slate solved the problem of pillars. It could not be cut rounded, so was dressed in an octagonal shape. Unpolished, blue-grey, lying on the ground, the 'pillars' looked as though I was about to create Kar-nak, but once in place were quite suitable.

After the conversion there were five bedrooms, one very tiny, and two bathrooms—all painted white with chintz curtains.

There were several built-in cupboards but more furniture was needed and I used to go to local sales; at one I was fortunate to get one armchair and three occasional rush-seated chairs for a total of four shillings.

There was a large attic which had the original farm grinders fixed to the beams. It was open over the joists and to the roof and a lot of heat used to escape. At first I thought to seal it, then it seemed ideal for a bedsitting-room for anyone who wanted quiet to read or write. So the roof was insulated, a floor made over the open joists, and a bathroom leading off and dormer window installed. The roof is quite high but slanting, and the recesses make good cupboards. The original beams of natural wood are uncovered and the rest of the room is white. In many of the houses in the neighbourhood the beams are of old ships' timbers. Here, though they have certain curves, they are just ordinary trees.

The attic has a lovely view across the bay, and I like it so much I have made it into my bedroom.

In the sixties I had a job in London and was away a lot of the time. Then I married again and lived at beautiful Firle in Sussex for twelve years. I think the whole of this house could fit into the great hall at Firle.

During those years a variety of people lived here. Most were appreciative and considerate, but inevitably there was a good deal of wear and tear and when I came back in 1983 it was very dilapidated and in a state of confusion. Egg-cups in the attic bathroom, lamps in the cellar, curtains in shreds, furniture in smithereens. Many objects vanished, including a very heavy doorstop, a copper nugget which my uncle had brought back from Alaska—travelling on foot, by horse and canoe in order to join up for the 1914–18 war.

Gradually the house is returning to normal, and is now much as before.

Diana Gage

The large attic is now a bedroom with a view across Morecambe Bay.

The hall is in pale blue, blending with the large tapestry on the staircase wall.

Cynthia Gladwyn

BRAMFIELD HALL
Halesworth, Suffolk

I knew that in the Middle Ages the priest at Bramfield lived 'a bowshot from the church', but recently our Suffolk architect Eric Sandon discovered from documents that this in fact was the house in which he lived. Hence our fish pond.

The church had become enormously rich since East Anglia, leading nowhere, had been spared the troubles of the Wars of the Roses. Then in the sixteenth century with Henry VIII came changes of religion creating dreadful destruction and burnings, so that finally the priest retreated to Mettingham College and the house was acquired by the Rabetts, an old family from the nearby town of Dunwich which was caving into the sea. They lived at Bramfield Hall (as it now became) for nearly three hundred years, until 1899.

The house they took over was a thatched timber-framed building with wattle and daub walls which they encased with Tudor brick. The great hall would have risen to the entire height of the building. Some modernization was done in the time of Queen Anne, including a new porch, but some time towards the end of the eighteenth century the Rabetts must have come into money

A pretty Venetian four-poster trimmed by Lady Gladwyn in the pale pink bedroom.

which enabled them to change its appearance completely. It was stuccoed white and the windows were altered. Evidently this work was carried out by men who had been employed at nearby Heveningham under Wyatt, since windows, shutters and chimney-pieces are almost identical with those on the upper floor at Hevingham. I mention all this because Bramfield is so often described as being an eighteenth century house.

After the departure of the Rabetts it changed hands several times until we acquired it at the end of 1945; we were able to move in early in 1946 with such of our things as had not been bombed and pieces of furniture and pictures lent or given us by our families. Serious redecoration was out of the question. However, there was a good deal of brown paint inside which was extremely darkening with the thick walls, and I remember being dismayed to find that, in those post-war days of austerity, there was no white paint, only cream.

At that time there was still alive a splendid craftsman, our village carpenter Bill Foster, who came to help and who told me much that I needed to know about the house; he had worked for one of the owners, Sir George Vernon, who was nursing the constituency just before the First World War. Bill Foster spoke the most enchanting old English, such as saying that a particular screw was 'not mighty enough' for the sconce he was 'offering up'.

And when he had painted the library yellow he said: 'That will smile at you when you come in.' Of more importance, he was a mine of information about the alterations he had done for Sir George Vernon, who had at once set to work to remove as many of the eighteenth century features as he could.

The white stucco was scraped off the exterior revealing the ancient mellowed Tudor red brick; the mahogany staircase was twisted round so as to give a larger hall and show more of the flagstones; old beams were uncovered; the Victorian chimney-piece in the drawing-room was removed to display the original fire-place behind. In the garden he planted yews.

In 1950 we were posted abroad for ten years, and on our return started making practical improvements and redecoration, now much needed. We employed the excellent firm of Reid of Aldeburgh to carry out this work under the advice of Eric Sandon. I chose all the colours. The hall and passages are duck-egg blue, blending well with the large tapestry which hangs above the staircase. Downstairs are fine old yellow curtains with good pelmets from my father's house in Norfolk. I am not so proud of the curtains to the windows above on the first floor. They are a beautiful old chintz with a bold floral pattern in strong blue, green and red, which I have known all

Bramfield Hall.

my life and never remember in pristine condition. Now they are literally in tatters. But I am attached to them, and four years in New York taught me how characterless rooms can become with continual redecoration. The library, which is at the north-west side of the house, is now a pale apricot and the curtains of the bow window are made of linen of the same shade with a bright red and orange floral pattern. These came from and were made by Spencers in Sloane Street. All the rest of the curtains were made by a wonderful old man, alas now dead, Mr. Comer, who came over from Lowestoft.

Now we come to the drawing-room, which I think is the prettiest room in the house. It is thirty feet long, being two rooms knocked into one, so we get cross-lights; the further end is where the original staircase once led from the great hall to the priest's room above his solar. The beams here are moulded, and an old legend has it that neither bats nor the devil can hang from them. The old fire-place greets you as you enter the room.

I have a predilection for pink, pale pink with a speck of black in it to relieve the crudity. It is a beautiful background for people as well as pictures. With this pink I always like an old-fashioned floral chintz with lots of stronger pink and green which I used to get at an excellent shop, Haynes, near Paddington Station, now unfortunately vanished. The sofas and easy chairs are yellow and other chairs are mostly pink. At the further end of the room, near the piano, is a purple velvet 'Madame Récamier' sofa and one or two other purple chairs.

The dining-room, on the left of the house as you come in, is still pure late eighteenth century. It has three windows looking towards the park and I thought that here we should have some strong colour for a change, so I chose a bright green named 'Gobelin green' which the workmen called Goblin green! The curtains are red damask from Peter Jones made by Mr. Comer. There is a very pretty cornice in this room and a fine marble chimney-piece.

Immediately above is my bedroom. I always have a pale pink bedroom and again a floral chintz, and, alas, a no longer white carpet—shooting boots and dogs have sullied it sadly. I love pretty beds, and my bed here is a Venetian four-poster which I bought in Rome, consisting of narrow gilded iron posts with gilded iron flowers at the four corners. On this I hung, rather than draped, my mother's lace, and nylon curtains. I have a splendid Spanish screen and a dressing table with a rather tattered old muslin petticoat which I cannot bear to change because it belonged to Lady Lee of Fareham.

My bedroom has three windows, and from

A view of the big drawing-room.

The late eighteenth-century dining-room.

where I sit and write I look down on the park and can see any person who may drive up. East Anglia was once an immense oak forest and we still have many fine old trees. My daughter and I have a mania for replanting oaks, and cherishing any small ones which appear in the rough grass. From my room I see all that remains of the celebrated Bramfield oak, a pre-Conquest tree which was a landmark in the thirteenth century and figures in an ancient ballad about Sir Hugh Bigod (who died in 1177). It fell suddenly on a windless June day in 1843.

The house itself looks lovely from the park. Within it is certainly shabby, but at least 'ça ne sent pas le décorateur'.

Cynthia Gladwyn

The large drawing-room has moulded beams and the original old fire-place.

Wilhelmine Harrod

THE OLD RECTORY
Holt, Norfolk

My house was built in the latter part of the seventeenth century as a rectory. It was unpretentious and rambling, but in 1725 a parson with grander ideas added some new rooms inside a pretty five-windowed front with an elegant doorway. Later, another parson diverted the stream which came from a spring on the nearby common to make a pond, and a rivulet which runs through the garden over a neatly cobbled bed. The clergy lived like country gentlemen then. The ones here planted fine trees, copper beeches, oaks and ilex, and a woodland belt for a Sermon Walk; and made

lawns and orchards and a walled kitchen garden. By the time we bought the house in 1962 the garden was very wild (more so now) and most of the paint inside the house was a dark chocolate colour; many of the rooms were distempered a very gloomy green. But in spite of the depressing decoration it felt like a very happy house.

It is the fifth house I have 'arranged'—decorated is too grand a word—and I have never thought of employing a decorator or even of asking advice. Not, I hope, from arrogance, but because it seems more natural to let things just happen.

The red-papered 'winter' room filled with books.

But I have been influenced by the taste of my friends: in the late 1930s by Nancy Mitford—my first drawing-room was pink and blue like hers; by Camilla Sykes, who collected black *papier maché* and lacquer, painted and inlaid with mother-of-pearl; by Roger Hesketh, whose knowledge of the Georgian period is unsurpassed; and by Robert Heber-Percy and Gerald Berners, who went in for fantasy. My houses have never *nearly* approximated to theirs but, nonetheless, their styles have always been, almost subconsciously, in the back of my mind.

We had to redecorate the whole house,

The Old Rectory seen from across the stream.

though we left (probably because the painters didn't notice) the ecclesiastical chocolate on the inside of the hall shutters, and I am glad we still have that. We were lucky about grates. There was only one hideous modern one which we had to remove; the rest are probably very late Victorian, not important but not ugly. The one in the drawing-room is surrounded by tiles with yellow daffodils on them, which was why we chose a yellow Morris wallpaper, plain yellow curtains and Morris chair covers in yellow and green. This is a very cheerful, light room, with two big windows to the east and one to the south, and it is hung with watercolours. I really prefer the room on the other side of the hall, done up much later after a burst pipe in the bad winter of 1978–79. This is a winter room, with only two windows, and it is papered in dark red (the Covent Garden stripe); most of the furniture, bought cheaply at local sales many years ago, is covered in red too. I

was lucky enough to get what was probably the only cheap lot at the Gunton Hall sale in 1981: a bundle of old curtains in striped rep, red on red, with which we covered most of the chairs. A lot of this room, which is semi-oval, is taken up by a big square piano, a Steinway, made in New York in 1878—not a pretty piece and so out of tune that it is fairly useless. It would cost far too much to put it right for a totally unmusical family, but we keep it because there is a vague rumour that it once belonged to Henry James, who knew my mother-in-law. I hate personal photographs anywhere except in my bedroom, but this old piano is very useful as a stand for some amusing old ones with family connections, of soldiering in India and such like.

Surprisingly, this room, though partially lined with bookshelves, was the rectory dining-room; surprising because the food had to be brought through the cold stone-floored hall. So we turned the rectory kitchen into our dining-room and the big rectory scullery into our kitchen. My husband hated kitchen meals, so until lately we have not tried to develop the popular kitchen–dining-room. I do not think it would work here anyhow, as I am such an untidy disorganised cook. I used to have a sofa in my kitchen for my friends to loll on; there are complaints because, to make room for a cupboard, the sofa has now been replaced by a large armchair. The back door leads from the kitchen straight into the garden, very convenient as I nip out to cut cabbage or asparagus while the water is coming to the boil on the Aga. Both kitchen and dining-room are passage rooms and get pretty muddy; the kitchen has an old, uneven floor of wide red pamments, but the dining-room is smarter, with black-and-white plastic tiles. It is perhaps the most successful room in the house; it is low, with a beam across the middle, and was probably the main room of the seventeenth century house. There are two windows facing north, and a glass door on the south side opening into the flower (as opposed to vegetable) garden. The walls are peacock blue, to match one of the colours in the printed curtains—huge scarlet poppies with bright green and blue foliage. When I saw the stuff at Liberty's I loved it, because as well as being a good design it suggested Poppyland to me, which was the name given to this part of Norfolk in 1883 by the journalist Clement Scott who, with Swinburne

The walls of the hall and staircase are hung with family portraits.

and his friend Watts-Dunton, often stayed on this part of the coast. Paintings look good on these walls, and there are either local primitives of boats and the sea by the Sheringham fisherman John Craske who died in 1943, or recent paintings by Jean Hugo, Barbara Robinson, Joan Zuckerman and Hector McDonnell. The old range must have been here as there is a wide chimney, and we bought for five pounds from some gypsies a long,

narrow naïve painting of Suffolk Punches, which exactly fits the opening. Victorian shell and wax bouquets under domes stand on the wide window-sills, together with bright bits of glass picked up for only shillings in the happy days of junk shops.

As a family we never throw anything away, and as none of the rooms is very big, my grand-children have made a museum in the attics. Here are toys, very broken I fear, going back for a hundred years; mementoes (gasmasks, ration books, etc.) from two world wars; kid gloves, spats, white silk mufflers, dance programmes, embroidered baby clothes, Victorian scrapbooks, and much more. Next door is a shell collection and a few old agricultural tools. Like Tom Kitten, my grandchildren, not content with many passages and five staircases, have climbed through trap-doors and explored the whole of the space under the rafters of the black pantiled roof.

Although the main road is very close, it cannot be seen from any window. The house sits right in the middle of its five and a half acres of garden and woodland, and in the spring the east and south windows look onto a sea of snowdrops. From the

The kitchen contains a large armchair for visiting friends.

dining-room and the kitchen windows on the north side, the view is, suitably, of asparagus beds and globe artichokes; and an old apple tree with a huge Albertine rose. Our poor young Rector who, with his wife and four children, has to live in a rabbit hutch, can hardly bear to make me a pastoral visit, so much does he covet the paradise which should rightly be his!

The low-ceilinged dining-room. A naïve painting of Suffolk Punches fits exactly over the old range opening.

Corner of Lady Harrod's bedroom.

A view of Lady Harrod's bedroom.

The drawing-room where the decoration was inspired by the daffodil tiles surrounding the grate.

Mary Henderson

South Kensington, London

We are back in a house we bought over thirty years ago. I still remember phoning from a call-box outside the house agent's office on the Brompton Road to tell Nicko, my husband, that I had made out the biggest cheque in my life—a two hundred pounds deposit (today, alas, this barely pays for a pair of curtains!). We bought our little London house—just before being sent to Vienna—in order to have a home, an English home, a base, an anchor. It has fulfilled this purpose.

Looking round it now I realise that it is very much a patchwork of our lives. The objects, the lamps, vases, plates, pictures, prints and Staffordshire figures, have been with us in our various posts, some acquired on the way, others brought from home. But they—like us—were surprised to find themselves arriving at Pauline Borghèse's palace in Paris (the British Embassy) and then unexpectedly being shipped to Lutyens' stately red brick mansion in Washington (our Embassy in the United States). Yet they fitted in quite happily and our guests found them—and us—'very English'.

The main bedroom where Lady Henderson has used material designed by Bernard Nevill.

One of the major drawbacks to our London house in the past was that, like most houses in the area, the bathroom had been added at a later date. It was built out on the half landing, next to the drawing-room. This meant that if the door were left open, a visitor coming to the front door would have as his first view of our home—a pink lavatory.

On retirement, we both decided we wanted bathrooms leading off our bedrooms on the second floor. After some trouble with the local city council and aid from our architect Nicholas Johnston, the work was carried out. The two rooms on the second floor became my bedroom-bathroom and an attic room and bathroom were added for Nicko; the old bathroom became my study, leading into a conservatory. This Victorian addition came from a new firm called Room Outside who deliver it in pieces which fit like Meccano. Our local carpenter installed it, carefully adding to the bold, white-painted arched windows three Victorian etched glass panels which we had found. The two on the door have a geometric floral design, while the larger square panel at the far end has a stylised urn filled with roses, tulips, convolvulus and fuchsias. Throughout the house early fads such as my craze for wall-to-wall red carpet and white paint have been thrown out. A stone-coloured cord, old rugs and glossy off-white paint have taken their place.

My new bedroom-bathroom is now a favourite room. Four old doors cut off the corners of the bedroom part, leaving it almost octagonal in shape with good cupboard space behind the doors. (The doors and the decorative, early stone religious overmantel were put into the rooms by a previous owner who was, we were told, a curator of the Victoria and Albert Museum.) The scale, of course, is minute, but it was just what I wanted to house my old polished iron bed, my eighteenth century angels (my first purchase in Paris when I was a correspondent for *Time*, before my marriage) and my travelling madonna—a present I have always kept with me since Boris Anrep gave it to me when he was working on the mosaics in Westminster Cathedral. (While I was suffering from vertigo, I remember the aged Russian artist climbing up ladders and stepping lightly on planks with the agility of a ballet dancer.)

The bathroom end of the room is like a Victorian picture album. The walls are covered with photographs—my mother as a young girl in

Bedouin fancy dress, my grandparents with my uncles and aunts stiffly posed with potted palms in Alexandria and my grandson's christening in London this year. These and others share the tiny space with my favourite Victorian paraphernalia. I had always wanted a *chaise percée* or comfortable old-fashioned wooden water closet for my bathroom and after a long search I came across a

A corner of the staircase.

rosewood chest of drawers. The top and the two front drawer panels lift up and fold back to become a seat. It was a Victorian commode chair which I have adapted. When closed it matches my Victorian hand basin with its rosewood cabinet base. Just above the chest of drawers is a large photograph of Queen Victoria sitting in a chair. She is pensive and dressed in black taffeta. How clever the Victorian dress designers were—a high neckline hides a sagging chin, a crisp little bonnet covers thinning hair, all so neat and proper. I bought her for two pounds in a market. Along the wall behind the claw and ball footed Victorian bath are antique floral tiles which Nicko has collected; they mostly come from old Victorian fire surrounds. I carefully chose which ones would go where. Some over the hand basin where they greet me in the morning, others on the far end of the bath so that I can see them well as I soak and think and choose my favourite flower. Sometimes it is the pale mauve pansy, sometimes the pink convolvulus, at other times my eye rests on the upright lily. Above the tiles a giant Victorian overmantel mirror repeats, reflects and gives a feeling of space. It was a monster to get up the stairs and I had to measure the space over and over again to make sure it would fit.

The decoration has been influenced by Bernard Nevill's design for the Lutyens gallery in

The claw and ball footed Victorian bath in Lady Henderson's favourite bedroom-bathroom.

A detail from the bathroom which is filled with Victoriana.

The small conservatory filled with decorative plants.

Looking from the study through to the sunny conservatory.

Lady Henderson's pretty dining-room.

Washington for the British Embassy Show Case which I helped to organise. Bernard used his curtains with William Morris rope edges, and tiebacks to cut across the vast long gallery—I have used them instead of doors between my bedroom and bathroom and between my bath and my desk. They are heavy and long, they have rope edges and lie well on the ground, making up for years of despair at the skimpy curtains supplied by the Department of the Environment. The material I have used was designed by Bernard Nevill for his Sekers Country House Collection. Bernard also had a covered window seat in Washington with a view over the Embassy garden—I have a tiny window seat, a view over London rooftops and space inside for my hair dryer! For the walls and double curtains I have used Laura Ashley's burgundy and sand ticking. It makes an ideal background for photos and prints, and I have also used it on photo mounts. Finally, Laura Ashley's lace curtains are a touch of the past and give me privacy, as does the little pull-down blind in matching fabric edged with lace.

Upstairs Nicko has a Victorian bathroom too. It was to be a shower-room but he preferred a bath and quite by chance we found a minute Victorian bath which is now surrounded with rows and rows of his favourite Victorian tiles. He also has a Victorian hand basin and water closet decorated with bunches of wild flowers. As the bedroom has sloping walls there are no pictures. Instead William Morris' hand-blocked briar rose wallpaper climbs up, over the ceiling and down the walls, encircling the room as in a garden bower. Pale apple green yacht paint has been used to paint the floorboards, and from his French window Nicko watches the London sparrows and tits fight over his birdseed nets which he replenishes at breakfast time. (The painted floor, although originating in this country, is an American influence and is used much more there today.)

It was the drawing-room that made us buy the house. We fell in love with its mellow Queen Anne pine panelling—so unexpected in a London cottage. Here pictures that have hung on other walls in other countries are now back in their old places. A naïve eighteenth century portrait of Darwin's grandfather (picked up in the Kings Road on our way to Chile), a Duncan Grant design for Lytton Strachey's library and a jug of flowers by Carrington look down on a large chintz-covered sofa and chairs. The crisp Baker's all over chintz is new. It replaces the more severe William Morris honeysuckle which we chose years ago when we were younger, and it is the material we selected for our private sitting-room in Washington. On the floor a Persian kelim and a Russian rug are both recent purchases. The Russian rug was probably a nursery rug. It has horses, dogs and birds, and our Staffordshire figures seem to like it very much; the dogs, I would say, are particularly happy.

As you leave the house, on the staircase landing there is an unusual clock. It is a picture clock with the Kaiser Franz and his wife at the opera. The last Holy Roman Emperor is glum, his wife, no beauty, is befeathered, with lorgnettes in hand; a deep red curtain and the two-headed eagle are the backcloth. At alternate hours the clock plays Haydn's 'Güte Kaiser Franz' (which was later adopted as the German national anthem) and a gay gavotte. Nicko bought it in Vienna as a present on the birth of our daughter Alexandra. After being turned out of two hotels because guests were kept awake by our baby crying, we spotted the clock outside an antique shop on our way to a third hotel. We quickly packed it into the car, and such was the charm of its music that Alexandra stopped crying and we were able to stay in the hotel without more trouble.

The simple, weathered pine front door and the blue and white exterior of our house are in sharp contrast with the interior, with its detail, its mixture of periods and jumble of colours. Somehow the new additions now seem as if they have always been there and the old parts of the house have a new and lighter look. The whole blends happily, perhaps because it mirrors a more mature taste and our feeling of contentment at being back in our English home.

Joan Holland

SHEEPBRIDGE BARN
Eastleach, Cirencester, Gloucestershire

Nearly forty years ago I would beg my husband almost every morning that, when exercising the horses, we could go to Sheepbridge Valley, three miles from where we were then living—Westwell, his old home where he was born and brought up. 'You can't want to go there every day,' he would say. 'I do, I could never get tired of it,' I replied; and now that I am here every day, I never do. The valley is intensely romantic and pastoral: the green hills are covered in sheep, there are beautiful beech woods following the natural contours of the land, while below runs the river Leach bordered in spring with white may trees.

The barn stands poised on the lip of the valley, and has a unique history for a present-day habitation in that it was one of the *mutationes*, or staging posts, during the Roman occupation. It is still known locally as 'the Roman barn', and we are the first people to live here since those days. Akeman Street, the Roman road running from Cirencester (one of the four largest towns in Roman Britain) to London, lies fifty yards below. The approach to the barn is down a line of eleven stone pillars, eight of which are classified as being Roman; and for this reason the colonnade is designated Grade I whereas the barn itself, being supposedly only seventeenth century, is Grade II. Walking around we have picked up innumerable Romano-British potsherds and Neolithic and Bronze Age flint artefacts all of which have been authenticated by the Ashmolean Museum and are now mounted as pictures in the kitchen. There could well have been a prehistoric habitation here. The configuration of the surrounding ground suggests that the Romans may have made use of the ditch of a Neolithic causewayed camp, and therefore possibly a religious site, when construct-

The approach to Sheepbridge Barn is down a line of eleven stone pillars, eight of which are classified as being Roman.

Above: *One of the decorative tapestry hangings which is in the main part of the barn.*

Right: *Sheepbridge Barn still retains its atmosphere of ancient peace.*

Looking towards one of the two massive fire-places.

ing Akeman Street, and that the Roman staging post was built within this camp. For those who believe in the so-called 'ley lines' we were told by a learned neighbour—somewhat of a mystic—that we live on a 'power point' where a number of important lines intersect. The children of one of our friends always call it 'the Magic Castle'! It undoubtedly has an immensely powerful atmosphere of ancient peace which we were afraid it would lose in its new role, but this has remained as strong as ever and is invariably the first feature that newcomers remark on.

We bought the barn, which had always lain a

mile or two beyond our own land, fourteen years ago from our neighbour Sir Thomas Bazley, who fortunately for us was finding the upkeep of it an unwarrantable expense on his estate and only wished to sell to a local man, who, as he said, 'was mad enough to buy it'. Indeed, all our friends were of the same opinion, which, when we looked at the tree growing out of the roof and the fourteen far-rowing sows wallowing happily in a foot of liquid manure in what was to be my bedroom, was scarcely surprising. We were tremendously fortunate in our architect and builder. The former, Michael Wright, a young man twenty-five years our junior (now alas dead) and educated in the most *avant-garde* architectural school, was the perfect foil to my husband and Alan Churchill, a local master mason, both of whom were steeped in the immemorial tradition of Cotswold architecture. Alan Churchill had his own, very small firm comprising himself and two boys.

The original building consisted of the main barn, sixty feet long by forty-four feet wide, which became our living- and dining-room, and a small adjoining stable fifteen feet by eleven feet—to be our kitchen—with no windows, in which lived a charming white horse. There were indeed no windows anywhere, and needless to say no fire-places. In order to build on further bedrooms at the back we had to get stone from two derelict cottages, as we were not allowed by the planning authorities to use any new materials. Heating presented a major problem. My husband spent two days at the Heating Centre in London in order to get the most expert advice, and they subsequently came down here to see the site and assess the situation. 'Do not worry,' the manager assured him, 'we will heat your barn like Ely Cathedral.' They finally settled for a somewhat less grandiose conception, that of digging four and a half feet below the barn floor and laying a honeycomb of copper pipes—in fact appropriately enough in the Roman system of a hypocaust—which though expensive to install is economical to run and has the added visual advantage of no radiators. It was naturally dark having only the wagon bays either side, so we elongated the triangular ventilation holes into nine-foot lancet windows which give a suitably mediaeval air; and our architect had the brilliant idea of making

The dining end of the living-room.

practically the whole of the north wall to the left of the fire-place into an enormous window giving a panoramic view of the valley, which inspired the remark of the French Ambassador when staying here, 'Every time you look out of this window you have your own Samuel Palmer'.

Our first priority was to retain the simple and massive feeling of the barn and to have an easily run home for our old age. Therefore we insisted, much to the chagrin of our architect (who had thrilling ideas of having our bedroom slung between the beams of the barn on mobile girders and approached by a rope ladder), on it all being on one level. We have just two self-contained suites of double bedroom, dressing-room and bathroom for ourselves and guests. We also wished to be warm, and have maximum security. To this end all the windows are double glazed. The doors are all treble locked, and some have security grilles in addition to other measures. The small kitchen has a hatch to the dining end of the barn, a wall-mounted oven and electric rings let into the working top. The decoration of the whole house can be very briefly described. There was none, we have employed no decorator, and have had only one idea throughout. This was to use just the colours of the surrounding landscape and the sky, and thus preserve the harmony of the building within its natural setting. The barn room has only greens and greys and yellows, which colouring is repeated in the planting of the garden seen through the windows. The bedrooms are all in varying shades of the blue and white of the sky.

When we bought the barn it was stacked to the roof with bales of straw so we naturally could not see what the floor was made of, which was just as well as it consisted of old railway sleepers and concrete. The stone floors from the derelict cottages came in very handy, but we still had to find more to cover such a large area. My husband had a great stroke of luck one day in Burford, our local shopping town, when he saw one of the old shops in the High Street being gutted and a monumental twenty-five-foot oak beam lying on the floor; this now forms the overmantel to the north fire-place. Concealing a drinks cupboard was no problem; we simply built into the four-foot thick wall to the right of the entrance and in a space eight feet by four feet have ample room for bottles and glasses, with a flower vase cupboard below.

We live entirely in this one huge room, and it is by no means a hardship. It is quite amazingly adaptable, and equally good for our annual charity concert seating a hundred and fifty people plus an orchestra (by a freak ratio of stone to wood to glass we happen to have perfect acoustics) or just the two of us in front of the fire. We built two massive fire-places, one at either end, which take enormous logs that stay smouldering through the night. Having both fires burning most of the winter we only need a minimal amount of heating except in the very coldest weather. The walls are hung with rather beautiful eighteenth century tapestries and silk hangings, but I have a very special sentimental attachment to the stags' heads all of which came from my parents-in-laws' forest in the Highlands where we spent our honeymoon. I can see them reflected in the monumental seventeenth century gilt mirror.

Over the years I have always managed to have those things I consider most important for a 'cosy' atmosphere, even though the vital elements of children and dogs, wood fires, flowers, candles and books have at times been somewhat on top of each other. Here, however, I have infinite scope to indulge all of them. The fires are vast, no flower arrangement is ever too big, books are everywhere, there are three pairs of altar candlesticks, the children have multiplied into grandchildren and the dogs are two immense Old English mastiffs. This is the most ancient English breed of dog, indigenous here when the Romans first came to Britain. They are our most devoted friends and never leave our sides. Other friends in the animal world are a flock of about seventy doves, dazzling white as they circle the barn on a sunny day—a great delight to us, but never more so than when they settle on the roof and their soft murmurings come through to us below.

The best times here are either the spring, when there are hundreds of lambs all over the valley, or the autumn, when the beech woods are at their most sensational; but the very best time of all is a still night with a full moon shining on the Roman columns, turning them from pale grey to pure white, when there is an almost tangible feeling of peace.

Joan Holland.

Betty Hussey

When young Edward Hussey, my husband's grandfather, decided in 1835 he no longer wished to live in the old castle in the valley, probably because it was both cold and damp, he commissioned the equally young architect Anthony Salvin to design him a new house on higher ground overlooking the view below. The result was a fine house in the revived Tudor style, built from stone quarried out of the hillside.

At the time the new Scotney Castle was built, it must have been the very latest example of modern planning. It boasted one splendid bathroom,

later made into two not so splendid ones divided by a partition through which one could hear everything. Since then we have added a lot more bathrooms. There was adequate plumbing throughout, and a central heating system (now converted to oil) in the main rooms which comes through iron grilles in the floor and works well to this day.

The Husseys were a very conservative family and did not like change, so when I first saw the house it had remained virtually untouched inside from the day it was built. Perhaps not all of it was lovely I must admit, nor indeed very comfortable,

The hall, a typical example of 1830s architecture at Scotney.

Above: *A bust of Princess Alice, a daughter of Queen Victoria, in the library.*

Below: *Salvin's library where books line every wall.*

Right: *A high Victorian bed draped in the original material.*

Above: *Mrs. Hussey's bow-fronted sunny bedroom.*

Below: *Corner of bamboo spare room with a handsome
eighteenth-century fire-place from the Old Castle.*

but it was a house with a marvellously happy
atmosphere, and above all it was eminently liveable in.

When my husband inherited Scotney there
was a lot to be done. Happily in those days we still
had our own estate yard to do the work, and as we
were already living in a large wing of the house we
had the fun of watching it all happen.

The first thing we did was to put the house on
the mains electricity, as till then the electricity had
been supplied by a grand old engine which chug-
ged away every morning, lovingly tended by the
family groom-cum-chauffeur. Unfortunately it

gave very little light and could not cope with any heating.

Then there was the water system. This was supplied by a spring which was apt to get rather low in summer, and as there was a lot of iron in the water both you and the towel emerged after a bath distinctly sunburnt in colour, so that had to be put on the mains too.

The kitchen was another problem—five passages away from the dining-rooms and enormously high. The upper half is now incorporated into what was our original wing. The new kitchen was moved to what had been the study, a very pleasant, sizeable room looking two ways. The view end of the room is painted coral colour and, as I eat there most of the time, is known as the third dining-room!

When all the essentials had been dealt with, there arose the problem of what to do with the rest of the interior and its decoration. We were determined that the character of the house should be preserved as much as possible, especially the library and the big dining-room, which are panelled in dark oak topped by the original Willement flock wallpaper.

The library to me is the perfect living-room. Books line every wall and there is even a book door. The curtains are a rather faded red serge, with very broad gold patterned stripes. All the furniture was designed by Salvin, and except that we imported some comfortable sofas and chairs, the room is much as it must have been nearly a hundred and fifty years ago. I kept to the warm red colours of the curtains and carpet, and the new covers of the sofas and chairs are a splendid red and white pattern called Ravenna, a design which I believe originally came from Lord Tennyson's home and was suggested by John Fowler. Some of the older covers are a trifle worn, but I rather like a slight shabbiness here and there!

The big dining-room was a trifle daunting. There were a lot of maroon-coloured leather chairs, very worn, the horsehair oozing out of them rather uncomfortably, so we got hides from a friend's deer forest in Scotland to re-cover them with. We kept the hides their natural colour, which is a lovely rich gold and lightens up the oak a lot.

For some reason there was a dearth of curtains in the house, but we were fortunate enough to acquire just what we needed at the great Ash-

burnham sale; the red moreen curtains in the dining-room and red Victorian bedroom are both from Ashburnham, as are the green velvet curtains in the hall.

The hall is really very handsome, but we thought it needed something doing to it. The panelling was a curious foxy red, which we had treated, and the fire-place had a smallish grate surrounded by shiny blue and white tiles. It also had its original velvet pelmet draped over it. Luck was with us, as we found a whole heap of marvellous fourteenth century tortoiseshell-coloured tiles lying in the old castle so we brought them up and used them for the rebuilt fire-place, which with its massive iron firedogs looks wonderful, and burns wonderfully well too.

The staircase walls were putty colour hung with numerous small watercolours, blue china and various strange weapons, while on the half landing one was greeted by a rampant, distinctly disintegrating boa constrictor! Weapons and snake now grace the old castle.

A friend of ours, David Style, found us some old rolls of a rather grand, bold patterned wallpaper in two shades of gold, the same period as the house, which looks well on the staircase where some of the family portraits hang. This is not an easy house to hang big pictures in—there is so much panelling, and so many books everywhere—but there is a unique collection of family watercolours from the beginning of the last century which hang in bedrooms and passages throughout the house. Almost all the family on both sides were very gifted artists, and the works they left behind are proof of their talent.

Out of more than twenty bedrooms, there were four particularly Victorian ones, with huge beds and furniture to match. Two of these we kept intact. One of the beds was designed by Salvin, and is so large I always feel he must have thought he was designing a house! However, my own bedroom, and several of the others as well, also my upstairs drawing-room, is furnished in lighter Regency taste from homes we had before we came to Scotney.

The drawing-room is a pretty room with a lovely view of the old castle surrounded by its moat, lying in the valley of flowering shrubs and fine trees below. It has a fine early chimney-piece which must have come out of the old castle when it was 'picturesquely ruined'. The walls are pale grey, the covers lime green and coral, which pick up the colours of the Aubusson carpet. The furniture is mostly black painted pieces, but pride of place goes to a handsome eighteenth century black lacquer bureau, filled with a fascinating collection of treasured family objects.

I have always known what colour schemes I wanted, what wallpapers and covers I needed for any particular room, and we were fortunate enough to have in our home town of Tunbridge Wells a friend and decorator, Merlin Pennink, who could invariably find, supply and make exactly what I wanted.

When we were moving into the house after the war good materials were still hard to come by, so I raided the linen cupboards and found lots of huge old damask tablecloths which I had dyed and used as curtains very successfully. For the same reason my bedroom was curtained with mattress ticking, now changed to something more glamorous!

One pleasant surprise was to find we had a lamp room full of good Victorian lamps still with the colza oil in them; needless to say these are now converted to electricity. An even more exciting find in a locked cupboard was a roll of a dozen ravishing eighteenth century original watercolours, labelled 'Birds and butterflies at the Brazils'. These now hang in the small dining-room.

We did most of the work and decoration in under six months, but naturally throughout the years other changes and improvements have taken place, such as making two or three flats for household and friends; the whole of the main part of the house, however, is still used and lived in much as it was when young Edward Hussey walked up the hill from the old castle to the new.

Scotney may not be one of the great English country houses, but it has for me all the warmth and welcoming attributes an English country house should have, and whatever we have done to make it easier for present-day living has still left it one of the most lovable and liveable houses I know.

A painting of the library by Billy Henderson.

An array of antlers overhangs the small back staircase.

Susanna Johnston

SHELLINGFORD HOUSE
Nr. Faringdon, Oxfordshire

People tend to groan when one admits to living in an old rectory. It's possible to experience the uneasy feeling of having fallen into some sort of trap; committed a whimsical solecism. Even if this confession does conjure up a horrifying obviousness, our rectory is jolly nice and suits us down to the ground. By lucky chance the house's name was changed when the last incumbent moved out so we can sometimes get away with it.

Shellingford House, stone-faced but partly rendered to protect it from howling gales trapped in the valley by the Berkshire Downs, was built in the sixteenth century. The front door and windows round it were added in the eighteenth century. Other excrescences are early Victorian. Fire-places must have been rearranged somewhere along the line as the house gained stature. In the dining-room we replaced a bogusly fluted wooden surround with a stone one, no longer of service in the tack-room. Behind each fire-place we could see traces of Elizabethan caverns. Alas, they were too big, too broken down and proved too much of an undertaking for resurrection.

The house has had few owners. Rectors lived

Corner of the drawing-room. There is a Victorian-added French window, and the ceiling is divided into elaborate moulded panels.

here for four centuries, until the moment when it was sold by the church in 1924. One of these clerics is good enough to visit us from time to time, providing the statutory ghost. Fortunately he is undemanding and seldom enters, preferring to peer through windows. Perhaps he was a bit of a snooper. When we arrived, the house had for many years been lived in by two elderly ladies. It had never been 'tidied up' and was fairly dilapidated. Our main and urgent problem was to rid it of the stench of cats. Burmese kittens by the thousand must have opened their eyes for the first time in every one of the twenty-odd rooms. I was tipped off—hyacinth bulbs were said to be the answer. I squeezed hundreds into tubs and lugged them into the slimy cellar—holding my nose until they bloomed. This, with the help of a general washdown and various licks of paint, did the trick.

I had no need to seek professional advice since I'm married to an incomparable architect. In fact he was the main problem: how to find room for his T-squares, drawing-boards, duplicating machines and various assistants in a house which would, but for this, have been the perfect size and shape?

The old ladies had cooked in a cupboard. The original kitchen, which looked out to a walnut tree and eleven garages (the ladies were rally drivers of high renown) through a three-light window with stone mullions and arched tops, had become the main maternity home. Hyacinths were screamed for. This is where we did our major work, hollowing out a space in an immensely thick wall under a chimney breast. Inching in girders to support the chimney, thus making a deep alcove, we had room at last for an Aga cooker. With unrivalled skill, Robert Keep of Pendell and Spinage, Stanford-in-the-Vale, carved cupboards from deal which he covered with white stain and a sealer, hoping to prevent them turning yellow. In this, happily, he was successful. Next door we built a pantry where washing-up goes on. The machine can thump away for all it's worth, while we're eating in the kitchen. Victorian bells, whose peals are now unanswered, remain in a high corner of the room reminding us of nurseries and dressing-rooms.

The old ladies' cooking cupboard was bare and I decided to bag it for myself. This met with opposition. It didn't seem right that any one person should hog any one room (other than for sleeping) in so large a family. I promised that if I

The refurbished kitchen with three-arched window.

A collection of china treasures in the study.

was allowed it I would write a book or something. I had my way, wrote a book or two, and honour was satisfied. The window of this room looks out, if you make a sideways squint, past a marble font where birds dip to drink, over a crumbling wall, to the downs, where on a clear day the eerie silhouette of the prehistoric White Horse can just be sighted. My desk is under the window with shelves, housing much-needed dictionaries, running along beside it. These were built, as were others in the house, with infinite patience at weekends and during long evenings by Martin Hedges, whose working day is spent repairing railway carriages in Swindon.

I had a length of curled-up wallpaper (left over from a former incarnation) almost large enough to cover the visible wall space. Even though these expanses were tiny, cheating came into play: paperless gaps behind sofas and chairs. It was well worth preserving this battered and faded floral pattern, reputedly a Voysey design which, I'm sure, the ghost must much appreciate.

Bearing in mind the dictum of William Morris that nothing must be on show in a house 'unless believed to be pretty or known to be useful', I decided to protect my family from the large number of my possessions which fall into neither category: to stuff them all into my study. Years ago I was walking through the town of Street and dallied outside a ragged junk-shop. In among the broken toasters I spotted a tiny china ambulance.

It was utterly moving (not literally so). Shiny white, no more than two inches high, it had a bright red cross stamped onto each of its side-doors. A peak jutted forward, halfway across the bonnet, and on its roof the multicoloured Royal Military College crest was stamped. My passion for First World War souvenirs was established. Now my room is lined with miniature aeroplanes, war memorials, Zeppelins, tanks, battleships and forage-caps. An awful lot has to be hidden away in there: insects from Peru, drawings by me, and orthodontal moulds of children's teeth. William Morris would faint were he to cross the portal. A chamber of horrors. He might cheer up, however, if he were to settle for a while in the hall and find himself surrounded by a wallpaper of his own design. Here he could sit in front of a good log fire

Personal possessions in the study set off by flower-patterned wallpaper.

and never complain that it wasn't useful in a house as ill-insulated as ours. It had been blocked up, but, with the powerful energy of Jack Fox of Russel Spinage, Faringdon, the old firewell was cleared out and a cement surround concocted with great ingenuity in imitation of a stone bolection.

Before leaving the Morris bower, perhaps I should say that although far too stingy and self-willed to dream of consulting a decorator, I am not proof against pinching the ideas of others. I spotted a sample of this golden leafy paper peeping out of a basket carried by my friend Amabel Lindsay, herself a decorator.

The best feature in the house, the seven-

teenth century staircase, rises from the hall through two floors in dark oak with immense newel posts. These strain towards each other but never quite meet. The steps are broad and shallow, the whole construction immensely sturdy beneath its balustrading and arcading.

The drawing-room (a good mixture of early and late) owes light to the Victorians, who added windows—two French and one bow. Coarse Elizabethan grapes divide the ceiling into elaborate moulded panels. The walls, rough and bumpy, wouldn't allow for a paper so we sloshed watered-down pink emulsion over them. To begin with I was nervous. So much pink looked like under-wear, but when the pictures were replaced and I had made a hideously expensive mistake in choosing sofa covers, it was fine. The dining-room, seldom used as such, is multipurpose. Here, again, we have built shelves where books of general interest can be used so that there is no real need for anyone to trespass in my sitting-room. In fact it's quite hard for trespassers to dream up an excuse.

Since I'm a compulsive bather and can't bear competition or queuing at any hour of the day or night, we added two extra bathrooms. Better safe than sorry. I was horrified when, sticking hazily to a budget, I learned that it was cheaper to buy baths with geriatric handrails attached in scooped-out slices each side of the tub. They seemed entirely depressing, but now—well! They're beginning to come in handy.

The house boasts a small back staircase. I'm told this is a 'must'. If by gruesome chance we have to sell, no Arab would touch the place with a bargepole unless he could despatch his womenfolk to upper regions by a route other than his own. These ladies might find it a little bloodcurdling, on reaching the top floor, to discover that the somewhat spooky nature of the wealth of black oak balustrading has been extended. On the long wall over the stairs we have arranged a collection of antlers. These were shot, decades ago, by my father-in-law. Warthogs, kudus and dwarf buffaloes from South Africa look glassily down on frightened guests and children as they cringe their way to bed. Fears are often enhanced by the scream of a screech-owl outside.

As an antidote to this creepiness my personal recipe for indoor jollity is that all clocks should be wound, kept ticking and chiming, and that as many fires as possible should be kept alight. A fire in the hall can give the impression of a warm welcome to unexpected guests however cold one's blood may run. Being a pyromaniac, I like to be able to burn things unexpectedly at my whim. Cigarette packets and sweetie-papers that find their way around the house look horrid in a wastepaper basket—worse on the floor. The television is also by the fire in the hall, but I prefer not to discuss this since it has been the cause of many a rupture—particularly at Christmastime—and might well prove impossible to burn.

Another view of the drawing-room.

The cheerful hall has leafy William Morris wallpaper and a perpetual log fire.

Loelia Lindsay

AN OLD RECTORY
Surrey

I sometimes lie back on my comfortable sofa and gaze lovingly round my room, murmuring to myself, 'I wouldn't change a thing—it's quite perfect'.

I ascribe my odious smugness to the fact that I built the walls around myself and didn't have to fit into other people's schemes. When you inherit or buy a house, the drawing-room is probably the room that has received the most attention and will be most expensive to alter, so that you may have to adapt or disguise; building from scratch, you should have no problems to face.

Three favourite pictures hang over the French bureau.

My chief delight in my walls has been their thickness, which makes it possible to disguise utilitarian comforts of no beauty; but more of that later.

The room is rectangular, measuring some twenty-six feet long and fifteen wide. It has one large window looking onto the garden. Two smaller windows flank the chimney-piece. One wall is entirely covered with books, though therein is concealed the television set, so well disguised by sham books that I sometimes give small children a prize for who discovers it first.

As I am only an evening viewer, my set remains nestling in the daytime behind volumes of Tolstoy, Pepys and Adam Smith.

The important focal point in a room is the chimney-piece; watch how on the hottest summer day people instinctively stand by the unlit fire. So twenty years ago when I built the room I was determined to have a lovely and perfectly proportioned chimney-piece (I still long to be non-U, and say mantelpiece). This proved anything but easy to find. I did not want a reproduction and could not afford a fancy one from a fashionable shop.

After roaming around I was in despair, when someone said they had heard of a good one for sale in a garage somewhere in Fulham. I managed to locate it and saw that it was perfection, but too expensive for me (a pittance at today's prices), so I walked regretfully away. Then I gave myself one of my lectures to justify an extravagance (with practice I'm good at that). I told myself that I would never find such perfection again; that the size, design and colour of marble were all exactly right for the room, that the drawing-room was the only room in the house that was to have a fireplace, and that it would be madness to pass by this chance. I hurriedly retraced my steps, which I have never regretted, and look fondly at it as I write. It is indeed true that one only regrets one's economies.

I had to change the design of the room to accommodate another lucky windfall which had come my way while I was still living in my big house. I had left one room undecorated owing to lack of funds. One summer I was motoring across Ireland to go and photograph Glenveagh Castle on the west coast, when I and the photographer, an antique-collecting buff, spotted a small shop in the middle of a typical Irish village high street. We stopped the car and nipped in. I wish, looking back, that I had bought everything in the shop as it was a treasure trove of unusual objects and the eccentric owner seemed to have no rhyme or reason in his pricing. Poking about in a dirty corner I unearthed four beautiful carved wooden curtain poles, with metal finials like pineapples and with all the original metal rings still on, painted white and gold two centuries ago. They must have come out of a very grand house indeed; I wish I knew which one. I bought them for a few pounds. They were not easy to pack and take

The television is tucked into the bookcase and can easily be concealed.

home, but I managed it. I vaguely hoped I should be able to use them in my unused 'banqueting hall'. I asked my gardener to stow them away somewhere and forgot about them.

When I started building the room I am now describing, I could not think of anything else night and day. How would my furniture fit in, what colour scheme would I go for, what material for curtains and covers? Suddenly I had a lightning flash of inspiration and remembered my Irish curtain poles, which were finally tracked down under a heap of potatoes. My architect, Mr. Ian Grant, had to alter the window positions slightly, but by joining two poles together they were made to fit the big window, while the two smaller ones fitted the smaller windows easily. The pelmets are sewn to the top of the curtains, and so roll back with them when they are drawn at night.

On one side of the main door is a French bureau and over it hang three pictures I am fond of. One is an amusing picture of a bulldog being painted by a monkey. The bulldog is hating his modelling session and has been given a glass of port to cheer him up and get him through his ordeal. Late nineteenth century, I found it in, of all places, Nantucket many years ago. Of roughly the same date is a minor French Impressionist of an absurdly overdressed lady pretending to fish, while her lover is staggering along behind carrying the oars. My third picture is different again; it is of

Above: *One wall of the drawing-room is entirely covered with books. Antique Irish curtain poles were fitted into the windows.*

Below: *Over the 'mantelscape' hang some of Loelia Lindsay's famous needlework pictures.*

a nymph goddess with attendant cherubs, painted on copper with a Verni Martin background.

On the other side of the door is a favourite piece of furniture of mine. I like to think that this little red and gold bookcase originated from the Brighton Pavilion, but I don't fool myself completely. I have travelled around with this slim little bookcase and was determined to move it once more to what I hope is its final resting place. I couldn't imagine where I was going to find a place for it in my overfurnished cottage, but was grimly determined not to part with it. Why I couldn't at once see that I had the perfect place for it I can't imagine. I had hardly entered the house when I found the ideal position, for apart from its charming exotic appearance, it is so exceptionally narrow that it does not stand out into the room, which is just as well as it is between the door and the bar.

The bar is the best of all my disguises; the

The marble chimney-piece, acquired twenty years ago, was an extravagance that has never been regretted. ☞

blameless-looking wall appears only to display a delightful collection of a little-known artist, Lelong. One can only surmise that the painter was very interested in food, as every picture has minutely painted details of enticing cakes, cups of chocolate and bread baked in the most curious shapes. Concealed behind this innocent collection of Lelongs is a very functional bar. There is a small refrigerator where soft drinks can be stacked and ice-cubes made and below is a stainless-steel sink, handy for mixing drinks, which serves the additional function of being an ideal place to do flowers. Under the sink is another cupboard for bottles which seems constantly to need replenishing. Flower vases live on the other side of the cupboard.

In this room I have displayed the best of my needlework. The guided tour will start with the needlework carpet, which adds splendidly to the room. When occasionally it goes off on loan to an exhibition for a few weeks, the whole room changes character and becomes drab. I acquired the design when I found in the Portobello Road a Victorian rug which was almost falling to pieces. I had the outlines drawn on a new piece of canvas and then worked my own colouring from the magpie hoard of wools I have collected over the years. I specially like the big sprays of lilac, which is an unusual flower to find in a Victorian design.

My best work I have grouped on the fireplace wall—a pair of bell-pulls which actually ring bells (though nobody comes) are judged the finest. I did them soon after the war when it was still difficult to get silks and satins. With the help of a kind friend in Paris and the Royal School of Needlework I designed exactly what I had in mind—a mixture of flowers, butterflies and big fat gourds worked to give an appearance of rough skins bursting open to expose their ripe seeds, actually beads of course.

The rest of my little pictures are individual flowers and butterflies; an exception I am fond of is a chameleon sitting on a branch of a flowering shrub in the act of turning yellow to match the blossoms. The chameleon is entirely worked in tiny steel beads, and the background is a deep verdant green. I have specially designed arc lights that I can turn on at night which make the beads glisten like jewels.

I will now describe my 'tablescapes', a new word that amuses me. Can one have a 'mantel-scape' I wonder? If so, I have one. I start in the centre with a very pretty blue and gold enamel clock, on the corners are a little pair of marble busts, and in between stretches a line of boxes of all shapes and sizes, dates and value. I hate glass-topped museum *objets de vertu* tables and like everything living free. Against the wall are a pair of Hodgkins, one picture of feathers and the other gulls' and plovers' eggs.

On another table on a stand is a picture of a deer's head painted by Simon Bussy, also a large ivory nut with gold leaves attached made by the celebrated jeweller Verdura, some mother-of-pearl boxes, a silver snail shell, a miniature of my great-grandfather, a somewhat battered Meissen figure, and last but not least a monkey dressed in full ceremonials, riding his horse sideways and holding a long curved-handled umbrella made of leaves.

On a still smaller table is a bead tray made by me. Inspired by one in the FitzWilliam Museum in Cambridge dated 1680, I determined to try to make a modern version. I was lucky enough to have the exact Sèvres blue beads to do my own initials, entwined like those of Louis XV and encircled by red and gold ribbons with bows. These form the mat at the bottom of the basket which started so humbly as an 'in and out' tray from Rymans. The net-covered sides are thickly encrusted with oranges and lemons, their leaves and flowers—quite a problem to make a bead orange; curiously enough you crochet it.

The remaining wall, mostly window, has two unusual shaped black and gold torchères; behind them on the wall are a pair of gilt Georgian mirrors and on the torchères stand a pair of crystal candelabra. Finally, in the centre is my overladen writing table, from which I am constantly distracted by the bird life in the garden.

In New York, I once asked a famous interior decorator what the fashion of the moment was. 'Serenity', he replied. 'And how do you achieve that?' I asked. By sweeping away all the clutter, he announced. But supposing the owner was very much attached to her clutter of personal possessions? His answer was, 'You don't suppose that I should let her ideas interfere with my creation?'

I should not want to be one of his clients.

Loelia Lindsay

Jean Muir

Kensington, London

Ten years ago we were living in a flat in Pont Street, full of colour, pattern, ornaments and paintings. Work was increasingly hard. I was dashing backwards and forwards from America, and as the pressure grew, so did the feeling that we should simplify the way we lived. The concept we had of a way to live that would balance the working life was, in a sense, a reflection of my love for the workrooms—the feeling of space around you, good proportions, decks cleared, a studio atmosphere and beautiful light.

As the feeling became a necessity, we began to look for more space and a friend who lived in the building introduced us to a marvellously proportioned flat behind the Albert Hall. It was rather grandly built by a Victorian speculator who ran out of money before the block was completed, so the story goes.

I do not remember that we consciously decided 'We will have a white flat', but that is what it seemed right to do. A good decorator painted it white from one end to the other. The walls of the biggest rooms are lined with a particularly rough hessian as a base for the paint, which gives a good

Ceiling-to-floor curtains veil the bedroom walls. The embroidered bedspread comes from Cyprus.

texture, and there are fine white blinds at all the windows. Alan Irvine, the architect and a fellow Royal Designer for Industry, led us to some good synthetic white flooring he found in France for an exhibition he was designing. It is matt and not cold to touch nor underfoot.

One day when the flat was ready, instead of going home to Pont Street, my husband and I simply came here instead and were joined by our housekeeper Carmen, who has been with us for fifteen years. All we had with us were our toothbrushes and make-up, and I don't think we went back to Pont Street for five or six weeks. By then, although our old flat held fond memories, it looked far too busy and complicated. We wanted to jettison our possessions, and very, very few things made the journey with us to Kensington.

Here we have only what we use: lovely bare white spaces and one or two essential and moveable pieces of furniture and a good kitchen and bathroom. What we did not want was ever to have to say 'This is the dining-room' or 'This is the sitting-room'. We have ten white calico seating units, designed for visitors to picture galleries, and these usually go along the length of one wall to make a long sofa though they are moved constantly. Our four tables, all alike, were carefully worked out and designed with John Minshure to be linked together or moved apart. Everything

The chair and double seat in the bedroom are in finely engraved Venetian glass, which catches and reflects the light.

Any colour entering the flat stands out immediately. The white calico seating units are constantly regrouped.

rolls smoothly across the floor—tables, chairs and the clinical trolleys where one stacks make-up or linen.

Once you have eliminated all the things you don't like you get down to the bare essentials and the formula that is perfect for yourself. Just as I begin a dress from the proper proportions of the body and resist additions, I have learnt to simplify my life in all directions. If, for instance, you don't want to come home to a clutter of letters, the way to deal with it is not to keep tidying but get rid of the desk itself.

The effect of the empty white spaces is to give a lift to any colour that enters the room. Food

The arched corridor runs the length of the flat.

looks wonderful in the flat, as do books, a pot by Fiona Salazar and Mo Jupp's sculpture. People also stand out—it worries some.

There are two ideas for the flat that we thought through but never completed. The walls of every room are wired for sound, but we never connected up the system. We had plans to project slides onto the walls so that we could have a perpetually changing exhibition of pictures. The one thing we did take enormous trouble with was the lighting, which consists of very small white spotlights placed at intervals around the picture rails, very similar to the lighting in the showroom in Bruton Street. There is a wide and very long arched corridor that runs from the front door to the far end of the flat, and in the evening with the lights turned low it has a cool, classical look to it which reminds me of Greece in late evening: calm, still and free.

The only large room whose purpose is immediately obvious is the bedroom. The bed has a white embroidered linen bedspread made by nuns in Cyprus, and all the walls are veiled by white curtains hung from ceiling to floor. These on one side cover the window, which shines through, and on the other hide a large built cupboard where I hang my clothes and keep my shoes and handbags. Clothes need to breathe not to be crushed.

We have only two pieces of decorative furniture in the flat, and they are both in the bedroom: a chair and double seat in heavy, finely engraved Venetian glass, bought from Christopher Vane-Percy and apparently from the palace of the Nizam of Hyderabad. They repeat and catch the varying lights. On the bed and the chairs are a collection of pillows and small cushions in lace-edged linen and cotton with embroidery and drawn thread work. Most of them were made in my workrooms by sewing together the traycloths I had collected over the years. It is Carmen's particular pleasure to keep these absolutely snow white and perfectly pressed. I treasure a white patchwork cushion made of tiny white moiré triangles starred with small silver sequins, a gift from a good friend, Naomi Langley.

Where a room has a function we wanted it to be completely efficient. A good, well-equipped kitchen and a comfortable, attractive bathroom were essentials. Harry and I are both good cooks and enjoy making our own meals, particularly

The tables are designed to be linked together and moved apart.

when we are in London at the weekends. The kitchen was the only room we thought out and planned in great detail, in consultation with a firm called Kitchen Planners. It was beautifully executed with a bank of well-finished cupboards, drawers and surfaces in black oak, and the central

Fine blinds on all the windows filter light into the flat.

unit accommodates gas, electricity and even calor gas, ready for any emergency. The equipment came from a superb German firm called Poggenpohl; it has stood the test of ten years and still looks marvellous.

To anyone who saw the flat in its original state, the bathroom would probably be the most surprising room. From a tiny, depressing closet it underwent an amazing transformation when we covered all wall and ceiling surfaces with enormous panels of glass, and found a wide triangular ivory bathtub to fit across one corner, making the most of the floor space. The step in the ceiling, which accommodated part of the structure of the building, adds to the effect of standing in a tall gallery of mirrors throwing reflections back and forward to each other.

The only other rooms in the flat other than Carmen's are a spare bedroom and Harry's dressing-room and bathroom, with a wooden sauna and a wall of books and more books—our great indulgence—opposite the cupboard where he keeps his clothes and fishing gear.

One aspect of the flat which gives me great pleasure is the evening light as it slants in and filters through the fine blinds. I love the perspectives of the view. Surprisingly close, you see the

details of the frieze that circles the Albert Hall, and beyond, the Albert Memorial lifts its spires above the trees of Kensington Gardens.

The life that goes on in and around the Albert Hall gives a particular character to our life here. When they raise the immense ventilators in the glass roof you can hear the music quite clearly. From our windows you can look down and see not only the musicians but perhaps the Boys' Brigade lining up with the band, the Institute of Directors, the Salvation Army or the Prom crowds. One advantage of living here is that if we go to a concert we can come home for a drink in the interval. How thrilled I was last year to speak at the AGM of that wonderful institution the Women's Institute.

From the flat, the drive to Bruton Street through Hyde Park, or to our new premises in Farringdon Road through Knightsbridge past Buckingham Palace, Trafalgar Square and along the Embankment, takes us through the heart of London. Depending on what time we leave, the park has a particular cast of characters. At 7.30 to 8 am there are the joggers, and sometimes the tramp with her suitcases of old newspapers. Half an hour later there's the man who does military exercises by himself in a corner of the Gardens, and the horses from the barracks being exercised in the Row, and so much more.

There are other areas in our lives where we accumulate and revise, but the original concept, to find a way of living at home which perfectly suits our London life, found its equation in this flat. We haven't wanted to alter it, we have resisted adding anything, and it has remained a perfectly satisfactory solution for ten years. When will we move on? Who knows? Instinct will tell.

Jean Muir

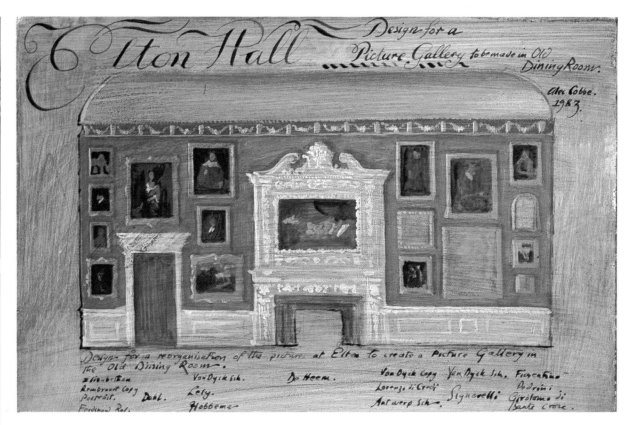

Meredyth Proby

ELTON HALL
Peterborough, Cambridgeshire

See p. 220
O.S. Historic Houses

When I married in 1974 we lived in London but were allowed the use of a flat at the Hall for weekends. My first memories of Elton are wonderful carefree ones since we enjoyed all the benefits while my parents-in-law had all the worries. I often found it difficult to understand why everyone was so gloomy on occasions, but when my grandfather-in-law died so many problems had to be faced that I could see why. The most pressing one was that, for tax reasons, we open the house to the public.

We came to live here in the summer of 1979 and decided to approach the problem on two fronts. Firstly, to organise the main state rooms so that the public could see them and secondly, to make ourselves comfortable in one corner of the house. This was not as easy as it might seem. Rab Butler is said to have complained that Elton was one of the most uncomfortable houses he had ever

stayed in and I think there was probably some truth in this.

In all our deliberations we were very lucky to have the architects Kit Martin and Bob Weighton. Kit was an old friend of William, my husband, and had been horrified to discover us 'lurking in the basement'. Since we no longer had the necessary help to cope with the original layout, we all agreed that we must move the centre of the household operations, that is the kitchen and associated rooms, up to the ground floor. Bob then spent many hours drawing up plans and we finally decided to put in a new kitchen, laundry room, cloakroom and playroom on the ground floor, new bathrooms upstairs, and to rewire and replumb with new central heating one complete corner of the house.

It was a great relief to see the builders move in in spite of the fact they stayed for nearly a year. We

The re-decorated State Dining-Room which was formerly painted in blue and held only five pictures.

Above: *Alec Cobbe's 1983 design for a picture gallery to be made in the Old Dining-Room of Elton Hall.*

employed a firm of local builders, Bowman and Sons, who are very experienced with old houses and all the problems associated with them. Although I have often described our house as a wonderful architectural muddle, it does have its advantages. Because it starts off in 1475 and rambles on in a delightful way until 1890, it means that there are numerous little corners and turrets which can be made separate from the rest of the building. It was into one of these corners that we retreated while general chaos was going on below.

Everything moved very quickly to begin with; demolition is easier than construction, but at last everything was ready for me to start decorating the rooms. I had once worked for an interior decorator in a very menial capacity, but my job had terminated abruptly when I rushed off skiing with my future husband leaving the company vehicle, loaded with materials, parked on a yellow line. I still had this unshakeable belief, though, that I might be rather good at it, and here at last was my chance to try.

I spent a lot of time rushing up and down to London, carrying little bits of material about. Then I was fortunate enough to come across Anne Harvey, who lives locally, who stocked most of the designer materials that I had been looking at and who could get everything made up. Here was peace at last and I spent many happy hours sitting at her house thumbing through endless books and changing my ideas at least twice a day. I had in my mind the sort of effect I wanted to create. Each room wanted to look distinctive and yet it needed to blend in with the history of the house. I am hopeless at drawing and have never done sketches of a room so I try to imagine the whole effect in my head. However much you plan, though, I think it is the final arranging of a room that can make or break a colour scheme.

It was quite a change for the house to have children living in it again. The last Proby children to be brought up here were the third Earl of Carysfort's family in the 1840s. Since then everyone had been so much older when they inherited that the nursery rooms were not really used unless children came to stay. It was once again necessary to organise the house properly for children. We did the kitchen, playroom, children's bedrooms, our own sitting-room and bedroom and bathroom first. These are essentially bright and cheerful rooms. Some of the materials are modern designed prints,

but the majority are traditional chintz and similar materials. The curtain designs are basically traditional, for example we copied our bedroom pelmets from a nineteenth century design book. We have suffered terrible problems with the proportions of pelmets and it is only by trial and error that one eventually learns. On our tall windows the most successful proportion of pelmet to curtain seems to be between one-fifth and one-sixth of the total height.

Carpeting was a terrible problem, since there was very little of what I call proper carpet in the house. There were endless little bits and pieces tacked together to make an island in the middle of the room, and corridors and bathrooms were covered with the ubiquitous linoleum. My early memories of winter at Elton are full of jumping from one piece of carpet to another in an attempt to get to the bathroom, where one always froze anyway. My answer to this particular problem was to go to the nearest carpet warehouse in Peterborough and order rolls of two or three different-coloured carpet and arrange a date for them to come and lay it. The difference to our corner was phenomenal. Suddenly, we were in a warm and cosy house.

We are now starting to decorate some of the rooms open to the public and our first project has been the State Dining Room. This faces north, and although it has a pretty view looking out across the park to the cricket pitch and Elton church, it is a cold room because of its enormous size (it is twenty feet high and measures forty feet by thirty) and lack of sunlight. It was added onto the house in 1860 but was built very much in the eighteenth century style. In contrast the Drawing Room, which dates from 1475 and faces south, is wonderfully light and sunny. The gilding and decorations carried out in 1860 in the French chateau style still have a tremendous amount of life in them. The contrast between the two rooms was so great that we had felt for some time we wanted to change the former, but we had been so preoccupied with making our own side comfortable that it had had to wait.

The State Dining Room was originally painted in a very deep purple-red and the dado, architraves, doors and eighteenth century fireplace were all woodgrained. The ceiling is very ornate and mostly gilded, and it had bands of different coffee colours and a sort of sludge blue.

We were able to discover most of this by scraping away at the various coats of paint. I do not think the room was changed at all up to the Second World War, but then the house was used initially by a girls' school and then by the Red Cross as a convalescent home. The State Dining Room became one of the many dormitories and the original decorations, except for the gilding, were lost under coats of washable distemper. After the war it was redecorated, but this time in varying shades of blue. Everything was blue, including the doors, dado, shutters and any piece of spare ceiling that wasn't gilded. Since the room was no longer used as a dining-room, it was turned into a museum for displaying books.

Apart from redecorating the room we also wanted to bring it back as a dining-room and display the books somewhere else. We deliberated for hours whether to put it back to red or whether to adopt yellow as the new colour. Among our friends, all the men wanted red and the women yellow. We had to take another very important point into consideration, and that was the hanging of many of our pictures. After the war five pictures

had been hung in this room and there was obviously capacity for far more. We had a lot of pictures sitting in a store-room and quite a lot hanging in rooms which did not show them to their best advantage. Alec Cobbe, who is a picture restorer and a friend of ours, had been pestering us for ages to redecorate the room and hang it in the eighteenth century style: that is, literally covering every available wall space with pictures. This we were very keen to do. A remark by Alec finally decided the colour as well. He was very definitely for red (silk if possible, otherwise paint would do), and when he heard I was still considering yellow he told me that the Duke of Wellington had persevered in a similar vein at Apsley House but as soon as his funeral was over the decorators moved in and changed the room to red. So red it was to be.

We were at loss to know who to contact about specialist paintwork on this scale but were lucky enough to be given the name of a firm who produced Ron Windsor for us. Ron is one of those chosen few with a superb eye for colour. He saved us from one disastrous shade of red and soon had

The recently repainted Marble Hall with the statue of Esmeralda by Romanelly dating from about 1860.

Mrs. Proby's bedroom looking through to the bathroom. The curtain pelmets were copied from a nineteenth-century design book.

The Yellow or Family drawing-room looking through to the Marble Hall. The Aubusson rug was acquired recently to cover bare floor boards.

us organised with the right colour. The invaluable Mr. Kisby, who lives just two miles away, did all the preparation and undercoats and Ron followed him, scumbling the walls and shading the woodwork. The whole effect was then varnished. We have chosen a different, warmer red to the original one and the dado, architraves and shutters are all in shaded off-white. The doors have been wood-grained again and were done by a local friend of Mr. Kisby's who came specially out of retirement to do the job. The ceiling was a tremendous problem. We left the gilding alone but still had to paint out all the blue. After various attempts at different coffee colours and off-whites we at last managed to find the right combination. It is slightly different to the original colours and probably much lighter. We have kept the same curtains and Persian carpet because although they are slightly worn, they are the ones originally made for the room and the cost of replacing them to the same standard would have been very high. The curtains, though, look almost as good as new since they were taken in hand by our great-aunt, Katherine Proby, who has done a superb job in mending them and putting them back to their former glory. One day we hope to restore the dining table, which we found in the apple loft, but at the moment we have to make do with another.

We have now also completed two more rooms, our own dining-room and drawing-room, and we are just beginning to feel at home. It has been nearly five years since we first moved in and I still look around and see so much more to do. I am looking forward to this and am rather glad that for reasons of cost and size we haven't just swept through the house with the same theme in one year. One of the most important things that has been achieved in the last few years is that we are at last beginning to feel it is our home as well as the Family Home. It takes quite a bit of time to put your own mark on four hundred years of predecessors and quite a bit of thought not to be too heavy-handed as well.

Meredyth Proby

The Grand Drawing-Room remains unchanged since it was decorated in 1860 apart from the recent addition of the rug and some rearranging of the furniture.

Didi Saunders

EASTON GREY HOUSE
Nr. Malmesbury, Wiltshire

There's a good reason why I was almost more frightened than flattered to write this contribution. For let me come clean and confess: I'm an American. And how dare I pose as an authority on the Englishwoman's house?

It's true I've lived in England longer than I've lived in America. And I find it hard to believe that anyone could love their English home better than I love Easton Grey. But I don't pretend to have lost all my American ideas or American heritage, and these are bound to have an influence on my home.

Maybe it was the crazy pioneering spirit—

like the one that took my ancestors bumping in a covered wagon to Minnesota—which had me believing I could take on a large, near-derelict house in Wiltshire which had stood empty for five years. Even my mother, who was pretty enterprising, thought it a mistake. When she first walked into the fabulous entrance hall, she said: 'You're mad.' I told her to keep walking, but that didn't help. There were so many rooms, big rooms; and so much that needed to be done to all of them. At the end of the tour, she was in tears.

But at the time I was hardly twenty years old

The drawing-room at Easton Grey House.

and—even worse—had fallen hopelessly in love. How can you talk to someone like that?

I still think, all these years later, that no one could have blamed me for falling in love. Easton Grey is a magical place: a calm, weathered Queen Anne house set in the countryside that everyone dreams about. Very green, very gentle. The river Avon below. And beyond, an unspoilt gem of a Cotswold village. All as English, as enduring, as Shakespeare.

There has been a house on the site since 1236. (Easton Grey was indeed mentioned in the Domesday Book.) And in the reign of Edward II, John de Grey held the manor keep in return for keeping one royal falcon in permanent residence for the king. Not a bad bargain. Later owners included Lord Asquith's sister-in-law, who entertained the prime minister for many summer visits; and the house was also rented as a hunting lodge in the nineteen-twenties by the Duke of Windsor.

One of our first decisions was to keep the bones of the house intact. Inside and out, it's hard to improve on those Queen Anne proportions; and who's going to interfere with an Adam fire-place such as we have in the hall, a free-standing light stone staircase with exquisite wrought-iron banisters, or age-old slate interspaced floors—even though they do take a lot of polishing?

It was in fact my husband Peter who made the whole thing possible. We couldn't afford to take on the house just as a home, but his business proved the lifesaver. The old Victorian broken-down kitchens were converted to offices; and though outside they looked—as they had always looked—a part of the old house, inside they dealt with his expanding mail order business in tweeds and knitwear. This was what helped to support our whole reclamation project.

A business interest may not be part of the traditional Englishwoman's approach to her house. But in this day and age, is it so foreign? Many stately homes are now open to the public; and no one denies that this may be the only way of keeping them upright and in one piece.

Another decision was to be the tortoise rather than the hare in our approach to the endless, echoing rooms in our new home. You can rush around wildly with gallons of white emulsion, trying to make everything presentable. Or you can take one room at a time and say: 'This will be the result I really want.' And although certain repairs to the roof and so on had to go ahead, and things like a kitchen and a bathroom could not be deferred, we managed to close our eyes to almost everything except 'the one room'.

The reason why the library remains my favourite is probably because this was the first just-the-way-I-want-it room. And for a while, it was almost a complete home. It was here that we played with our baby daughter, ate meals, worked on Peter's catalogues, talked to the plumber; here that I telephoned friends, quivered over bills and

Easton Grey House from the garden side.

estimates, and wrote to my mother to tell her she was right; here that I did just about everything except cook and sleep and have a bath.

If you came to visit me today, I think the first thing you'd notice about the library would be the great sense of light. There's an extravagant amount of window, including the later addition of a big bow window. This is where my overflowing desk stands. Facing south west, it catches most of the sun; and although I know this is a book about houses, not gardens or views, it's difficult to separate them. The garden, dipping down to the Avon valley, feels part of the room; and it's hard to avoid watching our pair of local swans, the kingfisher and the heron. Or to shut your ears to a very busy pair of woodpeckers.

Because of the natural brightness, we decorated in quiet, suedey colours: basically browns and beiges. And I must admit that one American influence was my stepfather's study in his Maryland home, Rolling Ridge. This was done in the most beautiful old green leather, radiating a kind of weathered warmth. And although we couldn't afford such a luxury, we tried to get the same deep, lived-in comfort with the suede effect.

There's a big bookcase, of course, full to overflowing—like my desk. It was made by our then gardener who, we discovered, was a lot better at carpentry than at gardening. On the walls, there are some modern French paintings and two spectacular wood carvings, St. Asprin and St. Agrippa, which once adorned the altar of an old church. They came from a client of Peter's who couldn't pay his bill and gave him the carvings instead.

The library faces south-east, looking down to the Avon Valley, and is always flooded with light.

The free-standing light stone staircase has wrought-iron banisters.

Looking through to the dining-room with its collection of T'ang horses. An original eighteenth-century Chinese wallpaper frames the entrance.

The library curtains have a strong geometric pattern, but still keeping to the brown and beige. I find them restful. They were designed by David Hicks, who has indeed helped us with many rooms in the house. So, too, has another great interior decorator, Tom Parr. And talking of interior decorators, I don't know if this is being American or not, but I've never found it embarrassing, or an admission of failure, to pick professional brains. The best professionals don't move in and dictate that everything must be stone-coloured or pin-striped or whatever. They'll have ideas, of course; but more than anything, they make *you*, the owner, think very hard and work very hard to get the colour schemes and furnishings and pictures and ornaments that *you* want to live with.

Peter and I have always found our advisers a stimulus, mind-stretchers. Added to which, they can be pretty indispensable when it comes to some technical problems. Most of us, for instance, are not used to curtaining big, nearly floor-to-ceiling windows. How should they be designed? What kind of pelmets? Frankly, I hadn't a clue; and without professional help, would probably have made horrendous mistakes.

But I can honestly say that if, after inspection, you don't approve of Easton Grey—don't blame David Hicks or Tom Parr. Blame Peter and me. Because, for better or worse, it's our taste, our choice. (David Hicks has indeed criticised us on occasions. When he last visited, he looked disapprovingly round the library and said: 'You're ruining this room with all your clutter!')

As we moved on, tortoise-like, from room to room we came on some unchangeable treasures. In particular, there was an original eighteenth century Chinese wallpaper, depicting a Chinese wedding. Like the Adam fire-place, who's going to lose *that*? It was just a question of some restoration.

But most of the walls and ceilings needed a fresh start; and it's hard to feel conservation-minded about old bathrooms or north-facing rooms painted a dark cream. In general, I think our starting point was nearly always colour. We didn't look at a room and wonder: 'Where shall we put our furniture?' The first question was: 'What colour shall we have the walls or the curtains or the carpet?'

Take our dining-room. (For many years a happy ping-pong room for our now four children.) When this became our next project, we began with a large Spanish carpet, woven to our design in Madrid, and everything else had to harmonise. I was delighted to find that an exact replica of some curtains belonging to my mother fitted in beautifully. So did our precious collection of T'ang horses. But that carpet was the boss. That carpet decided what was, and was not, acceptable.

In the drawing-room, we began with a blue-and-white colour scheme and a stippled floor. (This stippling—almost like painting a tapestry on the floor—was another American influence: the idea came from the south of the USA.) Again, it was a question of harmonising everything else with these priorities. Our rare, painted Chippendale mirror was welcome, as was much of the furniture recently inherited from my mother. And we chose some punchy black lithographs at Sothebys, partly because we loved them, but also because we thought they would look their best against the drawing-room's bluey walls. The grouping of chairs and sofas to make for comfortable entertaining, the arrangement of ornaments, small tables and so on ... all this was important. But it came later.

Moving upstairs, we allowed ourselves brighter, more daring colour schemes. I felt the reception rooms of an old English country house should remain reasonably dignified and traditional; but modern wallpapers, lively paintwork, brilliant Portuguese tiles (again made to our own design) transformed the bedrooms and bathrooms. The ghosts of former owners might blink a little, but it's all such a good antidote to the (frequent) grey English weather, I believe they eventually come to enjoy it, as we do.

There have always been so many things to do. Peter's mail order business has evolved into my Country Boutique and Garden Restaurant, still attached to the house, where I sell mainly women's clothes as well as china, glass and gifts. That alone keeps me busy; and I've often wished there were short cuts in dealing with the house.

Lady Caroline Somerset, in her enchanting contribution to *The Englishwoman's Garden*, wrote that, with a modicum of taste, gardens were easy to create but 'damn difficult to keep going'. With old houses I think we catch it all ways, because they're damn difficult to restore, *and* keep going.

The drawing-room's blue-and-white colour scheme and stippled floor dictated the rest of the decoration and furnishings.

Like old people, they need constant attention.

But I don't want to end on a hard grind note. Apart from the sheer delight of living in Easton Grey—a place which, all our visitors say, takes you out of time into a world very close to an English dream—there have been things all along the line for which I can only say, 'Thank heaven'. But a word of warning. *Be careful about falling in love with a house because it's dreadfully hard to disengage.* You'll get over that devastating Latin lover. But a house remains a lifelong pull on the heartstrings.

If I have to move on to another home, I know the pull will always be there. One way and another, I'll be back and back and back to Easton Grey.

Part of the decorative collection of blue-and-white porcelain.

The entrance hall of Easton Grey House.

Anne Scott-James

A Downland Cottage
Berkshire

It is on the face of it absurd that I, who am six feet tall, energetic and restless, should have elected to live in a doll's house. An open-plan studio, with plenty of headroom and space for frenzied pacing, might have been more suitable. But in 1938 I was driving with my mother among the primeval sheepwalks and small, secretive villages of the Berkshire downs when we passed a small, square cottage half-hidden by apple-trees with a board by the gate announcing 'To Be Sold by Auction'. I was about to be married, my fiancé and I lived and worked in London, and we had no money for frills, but I wanted the cottage quite absurdly. It went at auction for four hundred pounds, I was the buyer, and my mother lent me the cash.

The cottage was of brick and tile, built in 1807 (a workman had stippled the date into the chimney), was sited at the top of a small, steeply sloping front garden, and faced west. The view from the front door was charming. It looked onto a triangular green planted with nine elm-trees, with fields of rolling pasture and an eighteenth century farmhouse beyond; to the right, a group of cottages and a Norman parish church. The view is changed now, but not ruined. The pasture is arable (how I miss the mushrooms), the elms are felled, the farmhouse has been gentrified, and the

electricity and telephone people have joined forces to create what Betjeman would call a wirescape. But there are no new buildings, and the parish has planted limes to replace the rook-haunted elms. The church is well preserved, and the hedgerows still blossom with hawthorn, dogroses and sloe.

The cottage was in a primitive state, without water or electricity, and was densely populated with insects and mice; there was an outside privy and an insanitary well. I will not bore readers with the trials and tribulations which are common to all who convert old houses. I made a major mistake in trying to muddle things out myself with a local builder, and if I were starting again I would enlist an architect, but after much trial and error my home was ready. Of course, it has changed in the forty-odd years since I bought it, and I am afraid that neither the house nor the garden is as pretty as it was at first. I had to build onto the house when my children were born, spoiling the doll's house look, and later enlarged the garden to make room for hideous necessities like a garage and a tennis court (now a croquet lawn), but I still like my cottage better than any other house I know.

The two things I want in a home are comfort and a feeling of cleanness. To me, comfort means cosiness, a dreadful word, but I know no other— an open fire, plenty of lamps and electric points,

A nearby group of cottages and the tower of the Norman Parish Church as drawn by Osbert Lancaster.

masses of cupboards, lots of hot water, electric blankets, and a simple kitchen with a minimum of gadgets. I am terrified of machines which slice with razor-sharp blades and I would rather wash clothes by hand than endure the surge and thunder of a washing-machine. These amenities I provided from the beginning. The one comfort I have never managed to achieve is freedom from draughts, and in spite of a double front door and double-glazed windows in the living-room, the inquisitive south-west wind still stirs the papers on my desk.

By a feeling of cleanness, I do not mean the aseptic hygiene of a Swedish house, but rather the freshness of an English farmhouse. I remember with pleasure the whitewashed walls, polished churn and pails and blue-and-white china of a dairy where I was allowed to skim the cream when I was a child.

My style of decoration is, I suppose, a debased and poor woman's version of John Fowler. Of all the decorators of my lifetime John Fowler is the one I admire most, and I feel that his influence has outlasted other contemporary schools of décor, such as the crafts revival of the twenties and thirties. Who now wants tweed curtains or oak settles? I was lucky enough to see some of Fowler's first work in country houses in the nineteen-thirties and was bowled over by its beauty.

His decorations were, of course, of the highest quality and all were exquisitely made, every pelmet a work of art, but anyone could adapt, as I tried to do, the fresh, countrified atmosphere of his rooms. I remember well his ethereal use, in a Regency house in Surrey, of yellow with white, his striped chintz curtains and inviting chaises-longues, the muslin curtains and lampshades and candlewick quilts in the bedrooms—it is significant that many of his fabrics were cotton. I also recall an ivy-patterned wallpaper in the hall, bringing a feeling of the garden into the house. That house was my ideal and I carried its picture in my mind when I set about converting my slummy cottage.

First, being obsessed with lightness, I had the outside painted white, which was perhaps a mistake, for when it has to be repainted the climbers which cover the walls resent being taken down and pinned back again, and can take two seasons to readjust. ,

Inside, I made the rooms, most of which get no morning sun, as light as possible. Downstairs, there were two tiny front rooms divided by a passage, with a primitive kitchen and larder at the back. I knocked the two front rooms into one, making a living–dining-room twenty-five feet long and twelve feet wide, and had an oak floor laid by a local carpenter, which takes a lovely polish. Since I dislike dust-traps and clutter, I had as much furniture as possible built in, and think this is very important where space is limited. On one side, built-in bookshelves three shelves high run the length of the room, with cupboards let in for games, bottles and glasses. The shelves are, count-

The dining end of the living-room in 1958.

ing from the bottom, fourteen, twelve and ten inches high, so that books of most sizes can be accommodated, including dictionaries. On the other side of the room, a small sideboard was built in at the dining end to take care of silver and table linen. Then I whitewashed the walls and ceiling and indulged my taste for Fowler.

I made the curtains myself of striped chintz in cyclamen pink and white, bought a Regency chaise-longue for ten pounds in Dorchester-on-Thames and had it upholstered in yellow-and-white striped satin, and loose-covered two cheap and uncomfortable armchairs in pale green linen. I bought a white rug for the hearth. But my pride and joy was a refectory table for the dining end of the room, painted in white and apple green, which

I bought at the Colefax & Fowler shop itself for fifteen pounds. Six Victorian dining chairs found in the Kings Road, Chelsea, were upholstered in a green and white ivy-patterned chintz. So there was my living-room, mostly white, with fabrics in cyclamen pink, leaf green and yellow. I must add that I had very few pictures then, the best being an Augustus John watercolour, so I put one or two mirrors on the walls. I already had quite a collection of porcelain, some of it inherited and good.

The kitchen was improved as much as resources would allow, and the larder was just big enough to convert into a bathroom.

Upstairs, a corkscrew staircase led to two double bedrooms in front and a single room at the back, all small, but with enchanting views over farmland or garden. I left them structurally as they were, putting a basin with hot and cold water into each, as the only bathroom was downstairs. We were young and healthy then, and a downstairs lavatory was no drawback. I had roomy cupboards built into each room.

I had the bedrooms whitewashed and made striped chintz curtains for the two larger rooms,

The cottage in springtime.

The light, fresh living-room has simple white walls and built-in bookshelves.

spotted muslin curtains for the single room, tied with large pink ribbon bows. This room faces east and is the only one which gets the morning sun, and I often sit there at sunrise watching hosts of small birds twitter and feed. A favourite bird in summer is the goldcrest, which nests in the Irish yews, and in winter woodpeckers come to peck up insects in the grass. I must mention that all this white would not suit an arachnophobe, for it makes a showy background for spiders. The conversion was just about finished by September 1939, so my enjoyment of the cottage was delayed for several years.

Today, the cottage is larger, with more rooms and two bathrooms, but my taste in decoration remains much the same. The living-room still has white walls (I tried wallpaper at one stage, but it made the room look smaller), but the other rooms are papered, some with French papers, others with Laura Ashley. The stripes have retreated, and the living-room curtains are a sprawly flowered chintz, the couch plain green. I have more porcelain today and many more pictures. The one change I regret is that my green-and-white dining-table has been replaced by a round rosewood table which is too grand for cottage life. (I shall smuggle the original table back one day, for it is safe in our London kitchen.) The rosewood table was installed at the request of my husband, Osbert Lancaster, whom I married in 1967; he is a round-table man, liking to flick his *bons-mots* in circles. He made few other changes, but did design a characteristic Lancaster room upstairs for his studio, a diminutive stage-set with pine ceiling, William Morris wallpaper and curtains, red carpet, and Turkish and mediaeval *objets*. To gain space he had the inspired idea of building out an oriel window, into which he fitted his drawing desk and artist's materials.

Over the years, the doll's house has proved wonderfully flexible, and, thanks to building in and building out, I and my family have never felt cramped.

Anne Scott-James

The dining end where a round rosewood table has replaced the original green-and-white one.

Nancie Sheffield

SUTTON PARK
Sutton-on-the-Forest, Yorkshire

*p. 260
O.S. Historic Houses*

Sutton, which is a Grade I building, was built in the middle of the eighteenth century by Phillip Harland. The architect is thought to be Thomas Atkinson.

Phillip Harland was left five hundred pounds either to build a new house or improve the Elizabethan house already standing. He chose to do the former. My husband and I always thought the money must have run out, as Elizabethan panelling was put back in some of the third floor rooms while most of the other rooms have lovely painted pine panelling except where the Victorians tore it out.

When we had to leave Normanby in Lincolnshire twenty-three years ago because of its large size, we were delighted to find Sutton, which was all we were seeking: a house of medium size, facing south, with a lovely park, woodlands and a farm in hand. We lived in a small house in the garden for two years, only going back to Normanby on Friday to Monday, while we improved Sutton, making a new dining-room, putting in more bathrooms and installing a lift, as the middle block is of three floors. The dining-room, a major

 *The morning-room is panelled with stripped pine attributed to Flitcroft.*   Above: *Sutton Park from the garden.*

operation, had to be created by removing internal walls in the east wing, with the new kitchen and domestic quarters next door. I knew exactly what I wanted done and we were lucky in having a wonderful architect, Francis Johnson, to help us. He also knew all the good craftsmen, woodcarver Dick Reid of York and plasterer Leonard Stead of Bradford.

We were lucky that all the rooms in Sutton have the windows, doors and staircases in the right places. The doors on the ground and first floors are of mahogany. I think what made my husband decide then and there to buy the house was the beautiful plaster work by Joseph Cortese in the

hall, staircase and the library. We brought four marble chimney-pieces from Normanby which fitted in various rooms very well. As the house faces due south, all the main rooms are flooded with sunshine and look onto the terraced gardens we made.

As all the rooms had to be redecorated, we chose the colours and John Fowler very kindly came down and had them mixed for us, which he did brilliantly. Luckily he liked our ideas. He also did the hangings on two of the four-poster beds and the curtains in my sitting-room. The morning-room was originally the dining-room and has stripped pine panelling which has been attri-

The beautiful ornate plaster work in the hall, staircase and library is by Joseph Cortese.

The library is a bright comfortable room with its many armchairs and a sofa.

A small table in the morning-room displays some of the snuff boxes collected by Mr. and Mrs. Sheffield.

The four-poster in Mrs. Sheffield's bedroom with its elegant hangings by John Fowler.

buted to Flitcroft and was moved to Sutton from a house in Hull. The ceiling has a misty cloud effect which was suggested by John Fowler and which looks very well. There is a collection of treen made by my husband which I have added to. When my husband was alive we were both avid collectors and he contributed greatly to the collection of Chinese snuff bottles in the drawing-room. I started to collect nineteenth century beadwork and fine needlework which I turned into cushions. The morning-room leads into my favourite, the library.

As this is in the centre of the house, we made a window door with stone steps down into the gar-den. I am a passionate gardener and I adore plants from the humblest to the rare. We moved some of the bookcases, designed by Smirke, from the Normanby library and they hold part of that library. The chimney-piece also is one of those we brought from Normanby. I have a big log fire and club fender and lots of armchairs, some of them and the sofa with loose covers in a heavy cotton from Colefax & Fowler called Ravena; the design is in two shades of yellow. The curtains are dark yellow silk. They are seventy years old and my mother-in-law had them in her London house in South Audley Street. Sadly, they are starting to fall apart. The gilt carved cornices above the pel-

Mrs. Sheffield's favourite room, the library, has a window-door leading directly to the garden.

*The tea-room whose walls are painted to look like tortoiseshell
and ivory.*

mets we brought with us, and strangely they only
needed to be reduced in size a very little as the
windows here are so large. Two years ago I went to
Lisbon and designed and had made two large
needlework rugs in brown, coral and green; these
are laid on matting. The walls of the library are
brown and the bookcases and dado off-white. The
Cortese ceiling is painted in two shades of white.

Over the last twenty-five years we have collected Imari and early Chinese plates; these are
hung in the tea-room, whose walls we had painted
in the manner of the eighteenth century to look
like tortoiseshell and ivory. This room leads into
the hall, and opposite is the porcelain room. As we
both inherited small collections we have put them
all together in this room. The hall is north facing
so the staircase walls are painted yellow with white
dado and plasterwork to give an impression of
sunlight.

In my sitting-room, which is in one of the
wings leading to the Chinese drawing-room in the
west pavilion, we put one of the chimney-pieces
from Normanby; this was made by the famous

Pedro Bossi. Our son lent us an early nineteenth
century chandelier—the facets hang like a
waterfall. As it is impossible to hang a chandelier
from a plain ceiling we designed the plasterwork
with the help of Leonard Stead, which was very
interesting and amusing to do. We incorporated
some of the motifs of Cortese. The first design was
not a great success but the second worked very
well.

The drawing-room which leads out of my
sitting-room has a very rare eighteenth century
hand-painted wallpaper which has the signatures
of the artists who worked on it. This paper took
three months to restore. On John Fowler's advice
we picked out the plasterwork on the ceiling and
the cornice in two-coloured gold. Using the lemon
gold makes it look so much lighter. The white
marble chimney-piece came from my sitting-room
in Normanby and looks altogether better here in a
much smaller room.

We were amazed how well the furniture from
Normanby fitted into a much smaller house. The
lacquer furniture came originally from the Japan
room in Buckingham House, now incorporated in
Buckingham Palace and built by John Sheffield,
first Duke of Buckingham, in 1705. The original
architect was William Talman, who was a notori-
ously difficult man; the Duke had a disagreement
with him and William Winde took over, which is
rather surprising as he was not one of the leading
architects of that day. There is a drawing by
Giacomo Leoni which came out of the Japan room
and shows the original façade hanging in the hall of
Sutton. Most of the paintings also fitted in very
well, as there is a secondary staircase leading from
the centre block to the third floor with plenty of
wall space.

There are two things I feel strongly about in
interior decoration. I do not like close cover carpets in the downstair rooms, especially in the hall;
it gives one the impression of coming into an hotel
or a block of flats. Lampshades must be very
simple, pleated or plain in white or pale cream,
and definitely no fringes.

I love lots of plants in the house in the winter,
mostly white and particularly jasmin, narcissi,
scented cyclamen and hyacinth, because they
smell the best.

Margot Brigdon, who was the forerunner of
John Fowler, taught me to get a big scrapbook and
pin in pieces of material, wallpaper, carpet,

fringes, gimps, etc., for each room so it was clear exactly what the colour scheme would be. So much more convenient for matching things.

Sutton, which is open to the public four days a week from Easter to October, is less well known than the famous historical houses, but it has an atmosphere of being lived in and greatly loved which so many houses do not have. People can relate to it and not feel they are in a museum.

Nancie McD. Sheffield.

An early nineteenth-century chandelier hangs in the drawing-room at Sutton Park.

Janet Stone

Salisbury, Wiltshire

The dining-room, low-ceilinged and beamed.

Reynolds and I had taken ten years of intermittent searching to find our perfect Old Rectory in Dorset, and twenty-five years later, when I was widowed, I found myself in the unexpected position of looking for a quite different sort of house, a smaller one this time, and with rather more urgency. Partly because of my passion for cathedrals, I had decided I wanted to live in Salisbury.

I found this house quite by accident. I had been longing for the impossible: water at the bottom of my garden and a view of the cathedral spire. Bicycling across St. Nicholas' bridge I suddenly noticed a charming terraced row of artisans' cottages; it looked as if they backed onto the river Avon. Then I noticed a 'For Sale' sign. I turned round immediately and pedalled back to find out more from the estate agents.

First impressions were not so promising. It seemed to feature all my least favourite things. It was an old dairy that had been modernised by a builder in a 'ye olde' way that made my heart sink. It looked like the interior of a pub. Beams had been picked out in chocolate and the walls replastered in bumpy textured whirls. And I don't even like the genuine thing—the Elizabethan period has never appealed to me very much. But what a wonderful shock I got when I saw the two largest rooms, the drawing-room and the main bedroom above. They extended to the water's edge, and through the large bay window at the end of each of them was one of the most perfect views I have ever seen: the cathedral spire rising above the willows on the island opposite.

I bought the house in spite of the oak beams. The views (which included the mediaeval bridge of St. Nicholas and the unspoilt red-brick Edwardian terrace opposite) were too wonderful to resist. Also, the window shapes were right—not too big, but low enough, which is vital—and the situation is so incredibly quiet. To be so close to the city centre and yet only to be able to hear ducks quacking seemed almost too good to be true.

I have always enjoyed mentally reorganising and redesigning rooms. Although the mock

The bay window of the drawing-room extends to the water's edge, giving a marvellous view of Salisbury cathedral spire.

The drawing-room furniture is of pale, honey-coloured wood. A large tapestry on the wall has a charming story attached to it.

mediaeval interiors of my house were a bit of a challenge, I realised that several coats of paint would more or less obliterate the beams, and a new layer of plaster would smooth out the Instant Whip whirls. Then the house would begin to come to life. The other general problem was the floor. There was a surprising number of rooms, and long wide passages with acres of cement screed on the ground floor. Mollie Salisbury suggested the perfect solution: to lay fitted coconut matting throughout, downstairs and upstairs, except for the drawing-room and main bedroom which should have fitted squares of rush matting. I particularly liked the idea of rush matting because it echoes my courtyard of a garden, which is laid out in a checkerboard pattern of old paving stones alternating with herb beds.

The marble bust of Mrs. Stone's grandmother in a drawing by her daughter Phillida Gili.

The only snag was that it is not supposed to be possible to fit rush matting. But I persuaded the carpet-layer to bind the edges to stop it unravelling. The effort was worthwhile because it did provide the sort of surface I wanted—softer than tiles or boards—and the natural colour is the ideal foil for my furniture and curtains.

So much for generalities. I will now describe in detail my favourite rooms, starting at the front door.

The hall is microscopic, and filled with a large coloured print and a John Piper painting, both of Lichfield Cathedral, where my father was Bishop. The dining-room has the character of a cottage 'front parlour'—low-ceilinged and beamed—and is filled with small sketches and one large painting by John Piper of mountains in North Wales. The latter was painted on a memorably freezing expedition up Mount Snowdon; we watched while he used moss instead of the sponge he had forgotten to bring. The large round table is one of my favourite pieces of furniture. It is painted in dark green veined marbling and was rescued by me from my friend Richard Stewart-Jones at 100 Cheyne Walk when he was carting it off to the workhouse—'I think they might like it, Jan, what do you think?' Fortunately I persuaded him that our need was greater than theirs. The chairs, with black-painted wood and rush seats, are a relic from my husband's grandfather's school, Stone House. The curtains are hand-embroidered and are really part of the hangings for my four-poster bed.

One proceeds through to a hall where the marble bust of my grandmother stands gravely between two of my husband's paintings and to the drawing-room at the end of a passage.

The astonishing view across the river Avon to the cathedral spire, with the Victorian scene of sheep grazing on the island, is still the drawing-room's most remarkable feature. I decided to plan the room round the colours in my David Jones and Mary Potter paintings. These include a particular pink and green. By a wonderful bit of luck some curtains and a chair cover which I had brought from Dorset had exactly the right colours in them. They are both William Morris designs, known as 'Compton' and 'Pink and Rose'. I had the sofa covered in pale green linen with pink piping. All the furniture is of pale honey-coloured wood: the spinet, which was a wedding present from my husband; the lute, which was made specially for me by Dolmetsch; the Victorian work table left to us by Toddy Vaughan of Eton, the top of which is a checkerboard pattern of tiny cathedral views; the Regency cabinet, filled with my collection of cathedral china; and the round table in the bay window, which belonged to my husband's uncle, Christopher Stone. The wall opposite the bay window is furnished with my husband's collection of 1860s books, with their glorious gilt bindings. I think books make the best wallpaper of all.

I put a long richly-patterned Turkish carpet on the rush matting, and for the first time it is in a setting which does it justice. The standard lamps have modern umbrella-shaped lampshades with a bamboo design on them in pale green.

There were two flaws in this room, both created by the builder, which had to be overcome. The first was a mysterious recess in the wall, made to look like a blocked-up window. It was dealt with simply and beautifully by covering it with a large tapestry which hangs from floor to ceiling. It once belonged to H. E. Luxmoore at Eton, and there is a touching story attached to it. Although he loved it dearly, Luxmoore decided to give it to the Red

Framed book plate designs by the late Reynolds Stone.

Another part of the drawing-room.

Cross to help raise funds during the First World War. Reynolds' mother knew how painfully he missed it and organised a subscription to buy it back for him; it was replaced secretly on the wall where it had originally hung. But her ingenious

The richly-coloured bedroom is also a sitting-room and work-room.

plan was frustrated by Luxmoore, who had developed the habit of carefully averting his eyes whenever he walked past the blank wall. In the end he had to have it pointed out to him. He was so touched that he left it to her in his will.

The second problem was the complete absence of any fire-place or chimney. It was solved by installing a cast-iron log-burning stove called a 'Dragon', with a pipe that goes straight up to the roof through the ceiling and my bedroom above.

If the room succeeds in its effect, it is because of the mixture of colours and shapes which the furniture and furnishings provide; the walls themselves I left the colour I found them, magnolia white.

On the staircase are hung two of my favourite portraits, both large paintings. One is by Furze and is of Reynolds' grandfather, Edward Stone; the other is a self-portrait of my son, also called Edward Stone.

My bedroom is at the end of a passage lined with my husband's framed engravings. It is, I suppose, my favourite room of all. The views are, if anything, even better than those of the floor below; one is more aware of the curve in the river and the arches of the bridge. In spite of being a north-facing room it is somehow always filled with light; the early morning sun pours in on one side and sets through the big window on the other. The cathedral spire perpetually changes colour according to the weather and the time of day; after dark it is even more dramatic, floodlit against the black sky.

My purpose in designing this room, which is as much a sitting-room and a work-room as it is a bedroom, was to make it warm, rich and cosy. The furniture is all dark, including a Victorian screen, made by my grandmother Ellen Barclay, and my four-poster bed, which comes from Reynolds' family. I chose a dark, glowing design by William Morris called 'Grape' for the bed hangings and curtains. I picked out a plum colour from it and used it, piped with the dark Morris pattern, on the bed valance, the canopy and the cushions on the window seats. I chose two paintings by my husband whose colours are primarily dark green to hang near my bed. This room has one wonderful luxury—it has its own bathroom adjoining it. Unfortunately the builder's taste and mine were not identical. He had put in it a streamlined mushroom-coloured bath and basin, with matching tiles. Something had to be done. I commissioned my son-in-law, the artist and illustrator Ian Beck, to paint a mural all over the walls with a bamboo motif. The minimal amount of furniture is all bamboo and the whole effect is, I think, stunning.

My house is not in itself a remarkable one, nor have I spent a fortune on it. But I have tried to create a place where my family and friends can feel at home, whether they want to work or to rest.

Janet Stone.

Anne Tree

SHUTE HOUSE
Donhead St. Mary, Nr. Shaftesbury, Dorset

We live in the ubiquitous old vicarage. The Church authorities changed its name after the war to Shute House, but it is known to our friends as the 'Dripping Vicarage'. Shute faces north, south, east and west and the East Front has a modest classical front. The house has a curious format, being divided in two halves, the new built around 1720, the old being the remains of a sixteenth century hostelry. The parson who built the new half evidently had grander ideas than his predecessors. This modern part consists of four sizeable rooms, two up and two down and a big staircase lit by a large Palladian window. He must then have run out of money or died, as the old part of the house is modest.

I had little or no experience of decorating as I had moved to a large folly, Mereworth Castle, as a bride, and over the twenty years we lived there had only the odd bedroom to refurbish. My husband was lucky to inherit a lot of furniture and carpets from his parents and over the years his mother has given us endless presents of beautiful things. The decoration of our house was a mutual effort by my husband and myself, and I must add that my

The staircase at Shute House incorporating the vivid blue suggested by the skies in Giotto's frescoes.

husband has an unerring eye for colour and scale.

We started from scratch, the hall with the big staircase being the starting point. While we were househunting we visited Assisi, where we determined that in any future house we might own we must incorporate the wonderful vivid blue that Giotto used for his skies. To this end I purchased as many postcards as possible which included sky. When we bought Shute the staircase was the obvious place to use this blue. We asked Cyril Wapshott to mix the distemper. The colours looked truly alarming in the buckets; bright dark purple, emerald green and lots of brilliant blues. These were applied by sponge on a pale blue background. At first the walls looked like an abstract mural, but the finished ones were beautiful, if a little startling.

To begin with, we had no suitable pictures to

Interior of the drawing-room painted by Michael Tree.

put on the walls to break up the colour, but a year or two later I was lucky enough to acquire a large set of Chinese prints which do the job perfectly. We chose a modern carpet from Colefax & Fowler, made from a design in blue and orange on a piece of Chinese porcelain which was found by Tom Parr in the Wallace Collection.

To the left of the hall are two rooms: a drawing-room facing south, leading to a library through a jib door, facing north. The library was to be my husband's room, the drawing-room, mine. In fact we all live together in a muddle. For the drawing-room walls I chose khaki. I have always liked khaki, perhaps it is a lingering

memory of glamorous officers in uniform during my impressionable years in the 1939–45 war. Anyway, khaki it is and a jolly good background for watercolours and drawings. These we have in abundance spattered on the walls. My husband has collected McEvoy for years. They are decorative and delicate. A pair of mirrors and some mounted exotic butterflies complete the decoration.

On the floor I have coconut matting with fur rugs. I don't like wall-to-wall carpet—it reminds me of hotel suites—but our coconut matting was the greatest possible mistake. It is impossible to make a good job of clearing up a dog mess: you have to get busy with a palate knife and it still leaves a stain.

The curtains, or what remains of them, are very old. They were in a bedroom at Ditchley and are mentioned by Madame de la Tour du Pin in her diary, when she fled the French Revolution and took refuge with her Litchfield relations, the then owners of Ditchley. The curtains are now reduced to faded blue patterned Dress curtains, falling apart and frequently mended with copydex as they are too frail to sew. In the space left over are pale cotton Venetian blinds.

The drawing-room was awkwardly shaped, having a large immovable beam two thirds of the way across the room. This meant that the fireplace was not central. John Fowler had the bright idea of putting up two pillars under this beam, which made the room square, leaving an open annex at the north end. Here is my writing table, faded black-and-gold lacquer. There is a bookcase, lots of potted plants and a tree by a glass door leading to the garden. On the other side we have a coromandel screen, hiding both the door and the drinks tray, an ideal arrangement for those who think the hospitality of the house less than perfect.

We bought a blue, yellow and white French marble chimney-piece, large enough for a big fire and room for a clock and vases on top. On either side of the fire-place are a pair of gilt gesso tables, with Chinese lamps and vases of flowers. Two sofas face each other on either side of the fireplace, covered in gingerbread-coloured cotton, easy to wash and good with the khaki walls. The cushions are in different coloured chintzes, all with the same braid. On the floor is a large pale yellow rug with a rose border, and on top of that a polar bear fur rug.

In front of the south window we put a round table. It has a lamp and lampshade of pleated chintz on it. The tablecloth came from my mother-in-law, and is a winner. It is French and has life-size animals in fancy dress. They are copies from Granville's '*Les Scenes de la Vie Privée et Publique des Animaux*', published in 1842. Opposite the fire-place we have a pair of tables by Johnson, carved gilt branches of oak trees with marble tops; Chinese lamps, again on the table tops, numerous small Chinese fretwork vases, always filled summer and winter with flowers from the garden. I have a mass of flowers in the drawing-room, perhaps forty or fifty vases and, therefore, I do not feel the need to go out in bad weather. As far as I am concerned, the main fault with the room is that the sofas are not long enough to lie out full length and go to sleep.

I have my own little study in the old part of the house. Half the walls are covered with old panelling, sadly painted over at some time. In these panels I have stuck paintings of flowers and leaves from the garden which I have varnished. I have not yet completed the panels as, if I do not finish a painting at once, I have to wait another year to start again with the right leaves.

I collect paintings of animals dressed as humans. On one wall I have a pair of prints of Russian Bear soldiers fighting Napoleonic Frogs. On another wall I have cases of stuffed frogs bicycling, dancing and playing cards. There is also a charming pair of courting stuffed ducks. He wears a top hat, bow tie and binoculars and she has a hat, lace shawl and an engagement ring on her webbed foot. Over the fire-place I have mounted pieces of landscape marble from Florence, and a

A table in front of the drawing-room's south window is covered by a French tablecloth displaying Granville's animals in fancy dress.

fossilised fish which is either forty million or four-hundred million years old; I can never remember which. The curtains came from the Kings Road, nineteenth-century and velvet, with an intricate pattern in patchwork. The rest of the wall space is covered with bookshelves. The middle of the room is taken up with a huge modern writing table that I designed. I covered it with pictures like a Victorian screen. Often the pictures were donations from friends who cut them out from magazines. It has a cork top, a perfect surface on which to pin letters and bills.

I do not anticipate redoing the house and as the years go by I suppose it will get shabbier and more worn like its owner and the next inhabitants will then redecorate from scratch in their manner and their style.

Anne Tree

Above: Numerous small Chinese fretwork vases are filled summer and winter with flowers from the garden.
Below: In the study a large modern writing table is covered with pictures—often donations from friends.

A well-filled corner of the drawing-room with the door leading to the garden. ☛

Rosemary Verey

Met her on Garden Tour to England 1990?

BARNSLEY HOUSE
Nr. Cirencester, Gloucestershire

Our drawing-room with its archway into the morning-room is quite my favourite part of the house. I share it with David—and our visitors—but feel completely happy sitting there alone, reading, writing, doing nothing, sometimes thinking of the people who have enjoyed it before us.

The house was built by Brereton Bourchier, the lord of the manor, in 1697 on or near the site of the former manor house. It was built in excellent local oolitic limestone from a quarry on the edge of the parish, the same stone as was used for some of the Oxford colleges. The style was old-fashioned,

with mullion and transom windows. Three years later Bourchier married Katharine Brydges, sister of the first Duke of Chandos, a great patron of the arts. It is not surprising that with such good stone available and his creative inclinations Bourchier decided to build a bigger and grander house, more suitable for entertaining his brother-in-law, and the baroque mansion Barnsley Park was begun.

The 1697 house was abandoned by the family, and in 1762 it became the rectory. It was enlarged in 1830 when an attempt was made to make it look Tudor, and the William and Mary windows survive only on the garden side—luckily

Pale colours in the drawing-room blend with the woven rush matting.

where our drawing-room is situated.

When we came to live here in 1951 the two rooms I am going to tell you about were three: our drawing-room, which was divided in two by cream-coloured panelling, and the dining-room, with white marble fire-place, deep yellow wall-paper and heavy dark red curtains covering the 1830 bow window.

It was in 1958 that we made major structural alterations; we moved out and the builders moved in for the summer. The large old kitchen became our dining-room and erstwhile double doors between the old dining-room and drawing-room were released and opened so making a wide arch-way. The panelled partition was removed from the drawing-room and our three rooms were now opened up into one glorious space, sixty feet long.

We took out the marble fire-place and replaced it with a beautiful pine chimney-piece which David had cleverly acquired when the big house at Draycot Cerne was demolished. It has a central female mask and is thoroughly baroque. Another clever buy he had made was a splendid seventeenth century oil painting of the arch of Titus by Viviano Codazzi. It fits exactly into the space above the chimney-piece and the two together make a striking feature as one looks through the archway from the drawing-room and on through the arch of Titus. The early morning sun catches it and brings the picture alive.

The space was wonderful for children's games, Christmas parties and dancing reels, but at this point we made a series of dreadful errors. We economised on carpets, using existing rugs which could easily be pulled back for dancing. I was ignorant about colours and too busy with a young family to worry about 'stuffs', and would have thought it extravagant to seek professional help. This was the beginning of the post-war Fowler era and we were still 'utility'-minded, good material being in short supply.

We painted the panelling 'eau de Nil'; you can imagine how dreadful it looked. For curtains I bought seventy yards of apricot pink material at a sale in the Edgware Road. It went well with the 'eau de Nil' but definitely wasn't right in the Cots-wolds, and the lesson I learnt was that such a large expanse of plain material looked flat instead of lively. My one wise decision was to have the cur-tains made by a good firm. They were lined, inter-lined and padded in conventional style; more of

them hereafter.

Have you ever measured up a room for a carpet and considered the pros and cons of having either wall to wall covering or just an island in the middle with polished boards all round? My advice is 'Don't have the latter'. It is wiser without ques-tion to pay the higher price; you'll never regret the cost but you will always dislike the mean look of a shrunken-looking carpet. Two more mistakes we made—then I can get on to better things. We kept a much too big, uncomfortable and not even pretty Regency sofa. We imagined we had to keep it because it had always been in David's life. Also, I insisted on having a huge grand piano occupying far too much space; wherever we put it, it looked

The drawing-room at Barnsley Rectory before alterations.

overgrown and upset the symmetry of the long French windows. When at last we steeled our-selves to part with these we felt released and were able to start properly.

It was a shame that we had treated this lovely space so badly for so long and it finally came home to us when David Vicary became a friend and gave us advice. Make it into a light, long gallery was his suggestion, keep the colours pale but warm and use pretty flower chintzes. Make the room feel as though it belongs to the garden. There are so many windows it *is* almost part of the garden anyway. As I spend most of my time in the garden, the idea seemed quite natural.

The architectural features around which the decorating had to be done were a seventeenth century stone fire-place with moulded stonework, nineteenth century painted panelling, four large windows and a glass-topped door, all facing south east, and two French windows on the narrow south-west side, added when the Gothic verandah

The amber-coloured walls provide a good background for pictures.

Tablescape of seed pods below a leaf and butterfly collage.

Framed Chinese fans hang in the archway which both divides and unites the drawing- and morning-rooms.

The drawing-room feels almost part of the garden.

was built in 1830.

As this was to become a room associated with the garden, rush matting was the obvious choice. It was made locally, or so we thought, and we ordered it from a mill in nearby Stroud; it wasn't until it arrived that I read the label 'Made in Hongkong'. It has been extremely successful, never shows the dirt as everything possible falls through it, and has a nuance of pattern created by the way in which it is woven. Compared with good quality carpet it is incredibly cheap.

The curtains were the next problem together with the future colour of the panelling. Thank goodness David Vicary steered us away from pastel shades! The panelling was painted two whites, the mouldings completely white and the flat surfaces dragged with a pale biscuit colour on white. Now that dragging has become a common practice

🐦 *Looking through the archway to the 'Arch of Titus' above the pine chimney-piece.*

there would be no problem in getting it done, but in 1968 it was impossible to find anyone locally who could do it. The painter who was working for us was immensely skilled and eventually, after desperate telephone calls to the wonderful Imogen Taylor of Colefax & Fowler, he achieved it brilliantly. Every wall space, window shutter, door—and almost us as well—was dragged with two whites.

We chose the seaweed pattern in fawn and white for the curtains. It was a momentous decision involving a hundred and twenty yards of material and the curtains would either blend with or dominate the final effect. They had to blend.

Two lucky things happened. I realised we could cover the existing curtains, and as the curtain-makers could not be persuaded to do this I determined to tackle it myself. Fortunately I have always enjoyed a challenge and this one took most of April and the help of two friends, one aged sixteen and the other ten. We laid each curtain in turn on the floor and cut round them. We pinned and stitched and the ten-year-old kept us tidy and put the pins away. All had to be finished in the school holidays so we worked to a timetable, twelve long curtains in three weeks. I made the drapes later. I chose a design from Mario Pratz and with some old sheets and pins I finally arrived at a satisfactory pattern. Each one turned out slightly different and I definitely improved as time went on. The top corners have fat, punched-in 'cauliflowers' and by now these have gathered a considerable quantity of dust, but I dare not take them down as I would never succeed in putting them up again.

Imogen Taylor chose for us some really pretty 'climbing geranium' chintz for the chairs and window seats. David Vicary found me two old rosy-patterned curtains to make into a cloth for a large oval table draped to the ground and some unusual brown flowery chintz for a small round table.

The pictures have been entirely my husband David's choice, except for the piece of Chinese wallpaper which we framed and put over the drawing-room fire-place. We had endless difficulty in finding a picture to fit both the space and the mood of the room. This piece of wallpaper, the bottom section of a panel, is very decorative, with two black swans against a flowery background. Another important feature of the room is a glass-fronted bookcase made in walnut by Peter Waals, a

Dutch craftsman employed by Ernest Gimson, the Arts and Crafts furniture designer. It is fifteen feet long and has six bays beautifully made down to the smallest detail. What is amazing is that although it was designed for another house it fits exactly into its allotted space. The books inside it are especially precious to me—all on gardening.

Corner of the drawing-room with walnut, glass-fronted bookcase.

Sit in the drawing-room and look through the archway and you discover that the atmosphere of the morning-room is quite different. Whereas one is almost part of the garden, the other is very much an indoor room. There are open-fronted bookcases and all along the top shelf are pieces of seventeenth century blue and white Chinese por-

celain. The colour of the walls is 'Hot Sahara', which compliments and sets off the blue china beautifully. Surprisingly there was no cornice, and when this was added it made a great contribution to the completion of the room; my husband wisely insisted that it was deep and bold as possible.

Peter Hood helped us select the materials for the sofa, chair covers and the curtains. The blue of the china had to be repeated but not too strongly. My desk is in the bow window, and as I look out I have a good view of the garden and can contemplate what we will do next in an effort to improve it!

Many years ago Oliver Hill gave us a collage of skeleton magnolia leaves and butterflies and this sparked off in my mind the idea of making a tablescape with interestingly shaped seed pods which we have collected on holidays abroad. They are of every size and shape, some long and thin and others fat and round, and they live on a mahogany table under the collage.

David is always having good ideas and after our ruby wedding he made a blue table and a ruby table each side of the fire-place. The ruby side has the presents we were given on that occasion and the central feature is a charming ruby, velvet-covered workbox given to us by Alvilde Lees-Milne. Another of David's ideas was to have six of my Chinese fans framed with rich coloured backgrounds and to hang them in the archway between the two rooms, the archway which divides the rooms and yet unites them as one.

Rooms like clothes should remain in fashion, though good clothes like good furniture never become unfashionable, but it is essential that the style of the décor be in keeping with the architecture of the house and with the character of the people who live there.

Jane Westmorland

A SMALL MANOR HOUSE
Gloucestershire

We had lived in ten houses before we bought Kingsmead and each one in turn had been destined to be our home for life—where we brought up our children, sank our roots, planted our herbaceous borders, etc. However, for one reason or another we always moved on, until eleven years ago we heard that this particular house was for sale. Over the years we had known it well from the outside and had always coveted it. It must have been built around 1720 and can best be described as a small manor house. From the road all we could see was a particularly attractive and

friendly façade with a wonderful pediment over the front door and, unusual for the Cotswolds, the original harling which had faded to a beautiful colour. The house had the added advantage of proper sash windows.

When we were finally able to look over it we discovered that the original front door was not used; a side door opening into a dark and narrow passage served instead. This gave a most misleading first impression of the house, and when we finally bought it we immediately made a drive up to the front so that one now walks straight into the

The main drawing-room looking towards the garden.

heart of the house—a small panelled hall where, however hard I try to move people into other and larger rooms, everyone always seems to congregate. Maybe because this is where the drinks tray stands. The long passage we originally disliked has been knocked into an adjoining room where we keep the television, books and hopefully our children.

Fortunately, because I enjoy doing it, the whole house needed redecorating; but unfortu-nately, or not, we did not have the money at the time to do it all properly. Consequently during the years we have lived there we have made many changes. The major alteration—requiring at least three or four RSJs—was knocking down an extremely important wall to make a good-sized drawing-room. To me, almost more important than having this large room was the fact that by putting in French windows we could now walk straight into the garden, which in the summer is

Corner of the flower-filled drawing-room.

The small hall is a favourite congregating place for guests.

The lobby filled with garden accoutrements.

The shelves in the drawing-room are filled with books and china.

like having an extension to the house. Much as I love being indoors I always seem to want to get out, which is possibly why there are, to many people, including, I often feel, my husband, an almost ridiculous amount of flowers in every room.

I find it hard to describe how I decorated any of the rooms. Nearly always there were curtains, carpets or something from a previous house that had to be fitted in. I never really seem to have started from scratch, but basically I love all the old English chintzes—roses, ribbons, speckled backgrounds—linen materials, silk cushions. On the whole, traditional, easy to live with and not obtrusive.

Apart from pieces of family furniture there was always the portrait of John, the tenth Earl,

who, though wonderful to look at in his dark red cloak, is eleven and a half feet high. He is now in the drawing-room, up to the ceiling and cut into the skirting board. I am sure many people would feel he overpowers the room, but we love him. Also in the same room is a huge and once old-fashioned, but now immensely popular sofa. It originated in my husband's nursery and was once slept on in a London house we had by two of our greatest friends the night before the Queen's coronation!

As to getting the basic proportions of the rooms right, arranging the furniture and hanging the serious pictures, my husband is far better than me. I tend to mind much more about my clutter—the ornaments, the perpetual flowers, the photographs and the dog baskets always seem-

A pretty arrangement on a landing.

Part of a bedroom.